IRRATIONAL
MARKETS
AND THE
ILLUSION
OF
PROSPERITY

DON DEVITTO

Glenlake Publishing Company, Ltd.
Chicago • London • New Delhi

AMACOM
American Management Association
New York • Atlanta • Boston • Chicago • Kansas City • San Francisco • Washington, D.C.
Brussels • Mexico City • Tokyo • Toronto

This publication is designed to provide accurate and authoritative information in regard to the subject matter covered. It is sold with the understanding that the publisher is not engaged in rendering legal, accounting, or other professional service. If legal advice or other expert assistance is required, the services of a competent professional person should be sought.

AMACOM
American Management Association
1601 Broadway
New York, NY 10019

Printing number

10 9 8 7 6 5 4 3 2 1

ACKNOWLEDGMENT

Writing this book involved many long nights at home on the computer after the kids had gone to bed. Fortunately, I'm surrounded by a close family and several friends who encouraged me to continue writing long after the initial excitement of the project had worn off.

I especially want to thank my mother as well as my friends the Schwab's and the Baldo's for all their support.

TABLE OF CONTENTS

PREFACE

Is America repeating the mistakes of the 1920s?

Is our stock market on the verge of a collapse like the one that took place from 1929 to 1932?

Might the world economy degenerate into deflation and depression?

These questions demand our attention today, as some unique risks threaten our prosperity.

The raging bull market in stocks acts as a huge stimulus to consumer spending. Rapid rises in stock prices create a wealth effect, encouraging investors to borrow and spend freely. Many have forgotten that the stock market can destroy wealth even faster than it creates it.

Meanwhile, the explosive growth of the Internet is transforming our society in profound ways. For those who respond quickly, the Internet offers the potential of limitless personal wealth. Those who are slow to respond quickly become irrelevant in the new high tech world. For businesses, the Internet represents an enormously disruptive new force. The growth of the Internet will create wealth for some and destroy it for many others.

Very few American understand these risks. Fewer still are prepared for the consequences of deflation. Ultimately, the Internet will prove to be a powerful deflationary force in our economy. Very few Americans appreciate this risk. Fewer still are prepared for the consequences of deflation.

We all want to believe we control our financial destiny. Most Americans probably take this for granted. Unfortunately, we seem to be losing our grip. America, indeed the world, faces forces that threaten not just our stock market but also our entire economy. We're in the midst of a stock market bubble that in magnitude has few, if any, precedents. Our economy sits on a mountain of consumer debt, encouraged by years of easy money and virtually nonexistent credit standards. Across the globe, almost overnight currencies crumble, erasing years of prosperity and ushering in despair and depression. The deflation that has emerged in the Far East threatens to engulf the global economy.

Where will this take us? The optimists tell you not to worry. They claim that our stock market is fairly valued. They believe that our high tech economy will usher in an era of unparalleled growth. They promise that the weakness in foreign economies will have little impact here in the United States. They point out that mild deflation is actually good for our economy.

Above all, they insist that as long as baby boomers keep turning 50, the American consumer will spend, bringing prosperity to our economy and our stock market. What a simple and alluring concept! No wonder people embrace it. But is this optimism justified?

The truth is that the world is far more complex than we would like to believe. Demographics are just one of many factors that affect our economy. The American (and world) economy today faces a risk far beyond anything we've seen since World War II. The stock market has become dangerously inflated in spite of Federal Reserve efforts to suppress it. If the air comes out of this bubble suddenly, America will have an intense economic hangover. Deflationary forces will be unleashed, depressing financial markets and economies around the world.

What's most alarming about our present situation is that we have yet to face reality. The long bull market in stocks and low unemployment levels have led many Americans to conclude that we're somehow immune to these risks. A dangerous complacency has entered the national consciousness. America is, for lack of a better phrase, in denial.

The economic forces we face today are not without precedent. Economic trends in the 1920s were very similar, yet we're reluctant to acknowledge the striking similarities. Perhaps the implications of these trends are just too ominous to contemplate.

But we can no longer afford the luxury of simplistic optimism. If we remain in this state of denial much longer, we may well lose control of our economy. If history is any guide, it will take a long time to regain it.

1

INFLATION AND
STOCK PRICES

Americans today have more money at risk in the stock market, in both absolute and relative terms, than ever before. What truly sets this market apart from all other bull markets is the unprecedented level of participation by middle class Americans. The prior great bull markets of this century (the 1920s, 1950s and the 1960s) did attract money from smaller investors via mutual funds, but due to the explosive growth of 401K retirement plans, middle class Americans have exposed themselves to the benefits, and the risks, of the market as never before. Additionally, the advent of trading over the Internet has for the first time brought Wall Street into the home of the average American. Online trading is growing at a phenomenal pace, attracting hordes of new investors and speculators.

Most Americans make a strong connection between the stock market and the economy. The tremendous bull market of the 1990s seems to affirm the strength of our capitalistic system and validate the tremendous technological achievements of the past decade. Indeed, throughout history the stock market has usually been a relatively accurate barometer of the health of the economy.

Unfortunately, there have also been periods when excessive optimism and speculation caused the stock market to rise far beyond rational levels. When this occurs, the stock market poses a dangerous risk to the real economy. This happened in the U.S. in the late 1920s, contributing to the crash of 1929 and the subsequent depression years of the 1930s. Japan experienced a similar situation in the late 1980s, leading to a market collapse in the nineties, and a severe recession that continues still.

The question we thus must ask is whether today's stock market is an accurate reflection of a strong economy or an unhealthy symptom of excessive speculation.

My fear is that we are again witnessing a period of dangerous overvaluation in the stock market. Its ramifications reach far beyond Wall Street. The record level of public participation in today's market has positive and negative implications. It is a wonderful phenomenon when stocks rise, apparently spreading wealth throughout the nation. Inevitably, though, the tide will turn and stocks will recede from these overvalued levels. When this occurs the financial and emotional pain will resound throughout this nation, affecting Americans at all income levels.

The striking parallels between today and the 1920s begin with the trends in inflation and interest rates. There have been only two periods of secular (long-term) decline in interest rates in this century (see figure1-1). The first period began in earnest in 1921 and ended about 19 years later with the beginning of World War II. The second period began in 1982 and continues today. While most economists and market analysts are happy to point out the positive impact of low inflation upon our economy, they reluctantly discuss the negative ramifications of deflation (falling prices) for our stock market and our economy.

Analysts supporting today's elevated stock market refer often to the low inflation and interest rate era of the 1950s and 1960s. They conveniently ignore what can happen when disinflation turns into deflation, as it did in the 1930s (see figure 1-2). No doubt this omission is partly due to the fact that bearish analysts tend to have a short leash on Wall Street. After all pessimism is bad for business. No one likes a bearish analyst during a roaring bull market.

Figure 1-1 US Government Bond Yields, 1900-1998

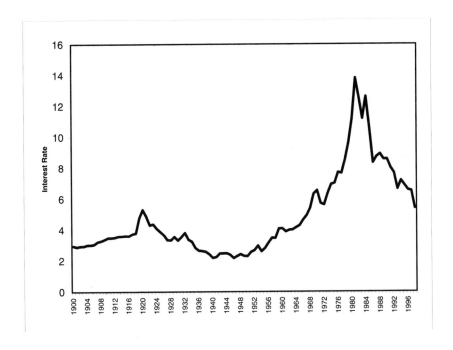

Source: Global Financial Data

Figure 1-2 Three Year Moving Average of Inflation
            (Consumer Price Index)

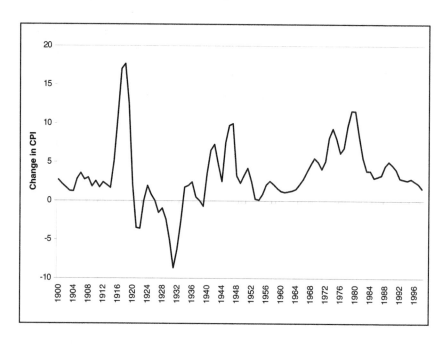

Source: Global Financial Data

What's the connection between interest rates and the stock market? It generally is accepted that two major factors affect stock prices:
earnings and interest rates. Clearly, rising earnings tend to support
higher stock prices and falling earnings generally depress stock prices.
However, interest rates affect the market inversely. As interest rates
rise, the market is negatively impacted: First, stocks have more competition for investors' dollars from bonds as well as other assets. As
interest rates on bonds rise, stocks become less attractive to investors,
so money flows away from stocks and into bonds. Also higher rates
tend to depress sectors of the economy that are dependent on lending
rates, such as housing and autos.

Obviously, these are important sectors. As they begin to weaken, earnings may suffer across a wide spectrum of the economy. The opposite effect occurs when rates begin to fall. Hence, stock prices tend to rise when rates are falling and fall when rates are rising. This basic concept lies at the heart of securities (stock) analysis and can be a useful tool in understanding stock price movements.

However, this general relationship between interest rates and stock prices doesn't always hold true. There have been long periods during this century when interest rates seemed to have little impact on the stock market. For instance, during the 1930s interest rates fell quite dramatically, yet the stock market was unable to overcome the impact of falling earnings. This same scenario played itself out during the 1990s in Japan, where deflation led to a collapse in corporate earnings as well as the market even though interest rates were dropping steadily.

Because deflation is such a rare beast, most analysts don't even factor it into their forecasts. They assume that earnings will rise eternally, with only very short interruptions brought about by intermittent economic contractions (recessions). These analysts would like us to believe that today's bull market has much in common with the low-interest-rate era of the 1950s and 1960s—but little in common with the low-interest-rate era of the 1920s. Few, if any, facts support this assumption. Furthermore, this overly optimistic appraisal of today's market is both shallow and potentially very misleading.

In the years preceding 1920 in the United States there was a significant rise in debt due to the costs of financing World War 1. As is often the case, this rise in debt was accompanied by higher inflation and interest rates. After the war the trend began to reverse itself. It was precisely this reversal that ignited the great bull market of the 1920s. Inflation and interest rates dropped steadily throughout the 1920s and the stock market soared (see figure 1-3).

Figure 1-3 Dow Jones Industrial Average, 1914-1998

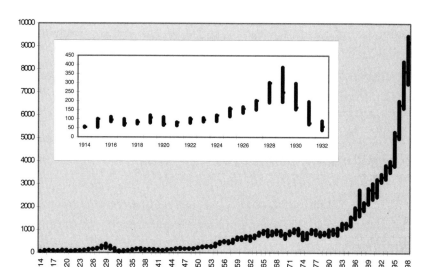

Source: Global Financial Data

The years preceding 1982 witnessed a similar sharp rise in debt and inflation. Beginning with the Vietnam War and spurred by the oil embargo of the 1970s, we began to see a sharp rise in inflation and interest rates.

Persistent price hikes led people to take inflation for granted and encouraged them to take on more debt. After all, it makes sense to borrow if you believe your dollar will be worth less in the future and you expect borrowing costs to rise. By 1979 the Federal Reserve Board (the Fed) realized that inflation was ruining the economy. Paul Volcker, head of the Fed, decided that inflation had to be brought under control.

The Fed initiated a severe monetary tightening that drastically raised short-term interest rates. It worked! By late 1982 inflationary expectations began to fall, and with them so did long-term interest rates. Once again, just as we witnessed in 1921, the stock market leapt forward. So began the greatest bull market we have ever seen. And herein lies the crucial difference between today's bull market and the bull market of the 1950s. Though rates in the 1950s and 1960s remained relatively low by recent standards, they *rose* throughout the period (see figure 1-1).

The higher stock prices and price/earnings (P/E) ratios of the 1950s were due to greatly increased confidence in earnings growth after the war-plagued 1940s and the depression years of the 1930s. Interest rates played no role in the bull market of the 1950s and 1960s. On the other hand, the fuel for today's bull market, as in the 1920s, is clearly the dramatic fall in long-term interest rates. Now, as in the twenties, the impetus for falling rates is the constant downward pressure on prices in our economy.

Financial markets and the popular press view this disinflation (prices rising at lower rates) very positively. However, are we in control of this deflationary process? This is the crucial question. Can we stabilize inflation at very low levels and maintain moderate economic growth, creating the nirvana economy that seems to be priced into our stock market today? Or is *dis*inflation simply the inevitable prelude to deflation, bringing with it global economic chaos, as it did in the 1930s?

The economic and financial parallels between today's economy and that of the 1920s are difficult to ignore (though many are succeeding in doing just that). The stock market, interest rates, and inflation rates are all following a very similar path to that taken in the late 1920s. While many may scoff at this notion, the risks are real. The 1997-1998 economic crisis that moved rapidly from Asia to Russia and Brazil gives us a clear warning that deflation is a disease that can spread very quickly. While the world economy seems to have stabilized for the time being, Japan and China are still fighting deflation. At this point no one knows whether these deflationary pressures can be isolated before they spread to our shores.

The potential for outright deflation exists for the first time in 60 years. To ignore this risk is to invite disaster.

2

DEFLATION

Until recently, the topic of deflation had received little attention in the financial press. This is not surprising; we haven't encountered it since the 1930s.

While deflation is typically thought of in purely economic terms, it also has a psychological aspect to it. *Webster's* defines deflation as "a decrease in the amount of currency in a country." No doubt, the monetary aspects of deflation are important. However to view deflation in a strictly monetary sense is insufficient.

In simple terms, deflation is a state of falling prices. This state may arise due to a lack of currency or money, a lack of demand for goods, or an excess of supply. Usually, it's a combination of all these factors.

What's critical to understand is that while the central bank of a country can to some extent control the supply of currency, governments have little control over the demand for goods, especially in today's consumer-driven economies. The implication of this is that once a state of deflation emerges, it can become difficult, if not impossible, for a government to reverse the trend. This is where the psychology of the consumer is so important. If consumers are reluctant to spend, the impact of government policy, whether fiscal or monetary, is muted.

Figure 2-1 U.S. Government Federal Net Outlays

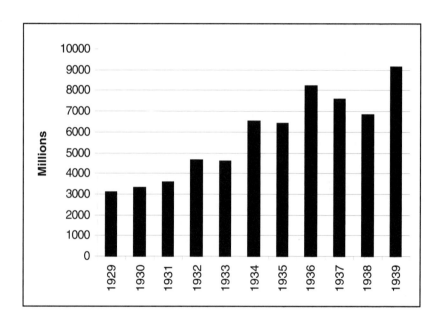

Source: Economagic.com

The U.S. economy of the 1930s and Japan's economy of the 1990s underscore the critical importance of consumer psychology: In both cases, governments used stimulative monetary and fiscal policies in an attempt to increase the demand for goods. In both cases, they largely failed. In the 1930s, America put its faith in fiscal policy to stimulate the moribund economy (see Figure 2-1). Government spending grew dramatically as a result of President Roosevelt's New Deal. In spite of this massive effort, the unemployment rate in 1939, nearly 10 years after the onset of the depression, remained stubbornly high at 17 percent. When the depression started long-term interest rates were already quite low (below 4 percent) and they continued to move lower throughout the depression years, bottoming out at about 2 percent in 1939. Short-term rates were actually negative for a time. Such was the dismal state of demand in America. Ultimately it was the beginning of World War II that finally brought America out of depression.

In the 1990s, Japan relied mostly on monetary policy to stimulate its economy. The Japanese Central Bank lowered short-term rates steadily from 1991 through1996 (see Figure 2-2). From 1989 to 1998 interest rates on longer-term (10-year) government bonds dropped from around 7 percent to well under 1 percent. In late 1998, the rate on six-month Japanese T-Bills dropped to a negative .004 percent, revealing yet another parallel with our experience of the 1930s. This is the first time rates in Japan have ever been negative. Yet, in spite of this huge decline in rates, the Japanese economy remains mired in economic stagnation.

Why wasn't the Japanese government more aggressive on the fiscal (government spending) side during this period? The obvious answer seems to be that until recently there was no sense of urgency. Though unemployment has risen in Japan, it remains below 6 percent—nowhere near the mind-boggling 25 percent unemployment that America experienced in the mid- 1930s. In addition, the Japanese have always been big savers. This trait serves them well. The large buildup of savings acts as a cushion against the deteriorating economy. Because of these factors, the Japanese government resisted any fiscal steps that might lead to a large budget deficit.

Figure 2-2 Japanese Discount Rate

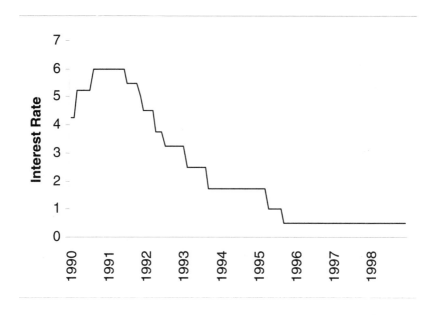

Source: Economagic.com

Of course, this attitude changed after the Asian economic crisis of late 1997. Japan is now taking serious steps to increase government spending and revive its faltering economy. However, there's no guarantee that this will produce the desired effect, as our own experience of the 1930s clearly demonstrates. All we can say at this point is that 10 long years after the Japanese bubble burst, the economy has yet to recover.

Some analysts will argue that in both cases it was a combination of previous policy errors and the tardiness of stimulative policies that led to deflation. Certainly, Japan's decision to raise consumption taxes in 1997 was a mistake, in that it led the Japanese consumer to retrench even further. Similarly, the imposition of the Hawley-Smoot[1] tariff in 1930 was clearly misguided, leading other nations to protect domestic industry and further reduce world trade.

However, we live in an imperfect world. Governments will continue to make errors in judgment. My argument is not that governments are powerless to prevent deflation. It's that once deflation begins, and once a deflationary psychology becomes ingrained in consumers' minds, government can no longer be depended on to remedy the situation. At this point, the fate of the economy resides in the optimism or pessimism of the consumer. This dynamic is what makes deflation so unpredictable and alarming.

While analysts may argue about what mistakes governments made in the U.S. in the 1930s and in Japan in the 1990s, the fact remains that both economies fell into a deflationary cycle after their stock market bubbles burst. In both cases, a full decade of monetary and fiscal stimulus failed to produce a significant and sustained rebound in the economy. The negative influence of the deflationary psychology of consumers overwhelmed the efforts of the government. Could the U.S. again be susceptible to a period of deflation in which consumers would dramatically cut spending, reduce debt, and increase savings? This is a complex but very important question. If the answer is yes, the implications for the American economy could be devastating.

While the U.S. economy is not currently in a state of deflation, we can no longer rule out the possibility. Inflation has been very low for some time. A shock to our economy, whether internal (such as the crash of '29) or external (such as the Gulf War), could conceivably weaken consumer confidence to the point that prices begin to fall. This has already happened in Japan (see Figure 2-3) and is now threatening other Asian economies such as China.

---

[1]The Hawley-Smoot bill enacted in June 1930 increased the tariff on imported agricultural commodities.

Figure 2-3 Japanese Wholesale Price Index 1995=100

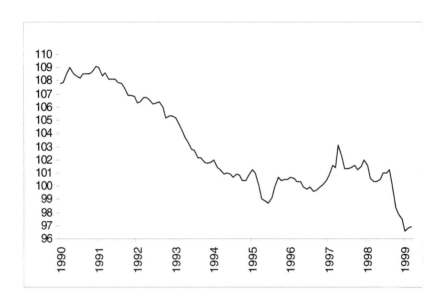

Source: Economagic.com

In addition to the risk of deflation, there are other disturbing similarities between our economy today and in the 1920s. Both eras witnessed a long period of disinflation brought about by improved productivity and the rapid development of new technologies.

Today's advances in productivity stem from the proliferation of
semiconductors in many consumer and industrial products, the widespread use of personal computers, and the adoption of new forms of
communication, such as cellular phones and the Internet.

In the 1920s, productivity was propelled forward by several inno-
vations. First and foremost, automated assembly lines dramatically
reduced the production costs of many consumer items, the most

important of which was Henry Ford's Model T. The development of the electric motor and the spread of residential electricity across the country led to an explosion in the demand for new household appliances, including vacuum cleaners, electric irons, refrigerators, and washing machines. Finally, the communication industry took a quantum leap forward with the widespread use of telephones and radio.

While many Americans probably think of the 1980s and 1990s as a period of unparalleled technological progress, in fact, today's productivity advances don't compare with the those of the 1920s. Between 1920 and 1929, productivity increased by an astounding 63 percent[2]—over 5 percent per year. Annual productivity gains in the 1990s averaged less than 2 percent. Though recent statistics are beginning to show some significant increases in our productivity rates compared with the 1970s and 1980s, it's too early to know whether these improvements can be sustained or whether they simply represent a short-term statistical aberration.

Perhaps productivity advances made today in communications and health care are not captured by current measures of productivity. Nonetheless, the undeniable fact is that personal income and economic growth rates today are far below what this country experienced during the 1920s.

What's the significance of the disparity between today's productivity growth rates and those of the 1920s? Optimists insist that today's astronomical stock valuations are justified because America has entered a new information age that will bring with it record levels of productivity and economic growth. But current economic statistics do not support this argument. Stock valuations are now significantly higher than they were in 1929 yet productivity rates are only now beginning to improve from the moribund levels of the 1970s and

---

[2]See Robert McElvaine, *The Great Depression,* Random House Inc., 1993.

1980s. Even if we assumed that America was about to enter an era of explosive economic growth comparable to the 1920s (a very remote possibility), the reality of 1929 and its aftermath nullify the assertion that increasing productivity somehow protects our economy from rampant financial speculation. In fact, it's increasingly obvious that today's new technologies (Internet trading) are facilitating speculation on a scale this country has never before seen.

The undeniable technological progress made in both the 1920s and the 1990s has significance beyond the economic consequences. The progress achieved in the 1920s may well explain the apparent confidence, perhaps overconfidence, for which that era is well known. Judging by the irrepressible consumer spending habits of the average American, that confidence is present again today. Perhaps the optimism we see today will prove justified. However, I suspect that when we look back from a distance on the 1990s, the conclusion will be unavoidable that, once again, overconfidence led to reckless financial speculation and that surging optimism led consumers to live beyond their means.

While the consumer-spending habits of the 1920s may seem tame by today's standards, a dramatic change did take place then. Until the 1920s, consumer credit was rare indeed. If you wanted to buy something, you paid cash. This conservative attitude began to change in the 1920s with the introduction of installment credit. For the first time, people began to buy cars and a host of other items on credit. The introduction of credit spurred consumption. However, the optimism of the 1920s came to an end with the crash of 1929. Consumers became more conservative; the result was a sharp contraction in the economy.

Consumption, of course, is essential to all healthy economies. In moderation, it's welcome. However, when consumption is fueled mainly by increased credit (debt) rather than by rising incomes, it creates a problem. Just as excessive valuations pose a risk to stock markets, excessive consumption poses a risk to the real economy. The greater the excess, the greater the risk.

This is what makes our current situation so precarious. The ease of credit in today's consumer-driven economy has dangerous implications. The average American is encouraged as never before to leverage his or her income with credit card debt, and leverage his or her home with home equity debt (see Figure 2-4). Many Americans oblige themselves to this easy financing and consume beyond their means.

Figure 2-4 Equity in Household Real Estate

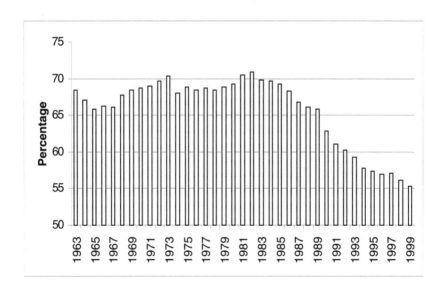

Source: Federal Reserve Statistics

Virtually all Americans constantly receive credit card solicitations by mail or phone, and now over the Internet. Barely a day goes by when we don't receive one, two, even three of these offers. Many say we're "pre-approved" for a credit line of anywhere from $2,500 to $100,000. Just today, I received an offer for a credit card with a fixed annual rate of 5.99 percent and no annual fee. That's quite an attractive offer when you consider that the prime rate is over 8 percent and 30-year Treasury bond yields 6.3 percent!

Banks are not only making it very easy to borrow, but in many cases, they're also offering very favorable terms. And judging by the tremendous growth in credit card and home equity loans, it appears that many consumers are having a hard time saying "no." To the casual observer this may not sound like such a bad thing. After all, if banks are lending, consumers are borrowing, and the economy is strong, then everybody should be happy. But there's a downside to this scenario: What if the borrowing and spending habits of Americans are temporarily inflated to the point where our debt becomes excessive relative to our incomes?

Clearly, our banking system operates on the assumption that most Americans will behave rationally and responsibly in responding to these credit card offers. But what if the "average" American has become overly optimistic about his financial condition due to the soaring stock market? Could Americans be excessively dependent on credit in order to maintain current levels of consumer spending?

No one can answer this question with certainty. Only during the next economic downturn will we discover the answer. However, the behavior of the stock market over the last several years should lead us to ask another question: Are we really as rational as we think?

In the 1990s, stock market valuations in the U.S. soared, far sur-passing prior bull market peaks. Just five years ago, the vast majority of analysts would have deemed today's valuations absurd. Virtually no one would have dreamed that investors would be willing to pay 40, 50, or even 60 times earnings for large, mature companies like Coca Cola or Gillette, let alone 80 to 100 times earnings for prominent technolo-gy companies like Dell and Cisco. Are investors responding rational-ly to our economic environment? Or have they simply become too optimistic?

Not long ago stock splits were deemed essentially irrelevant to the price of a stock. In other words, the value of a corporation does not change simply because it decides to split its stock. Yet, today it's not uncommon to see a stock rise 10, 20, or even 30 percent on the announcement of a stock split.

Clearly, these split-related price jumps represent irrational behav-ior. Indeed, the evidence of irrational behavior in today's stock market is simply overwhelming. When this long bull market finally ends, we're likely to reach two unavoidable conclusions: (1) Investors great-ly underestimated the risk of the stock market and (2) consumers often overestimated their ability to pay off debt.

The combined excesses we face in our stock market and the real economy (in the form of consumer debt) are unparalleled in modern history. They pose a huge risk to our society. But what causes an econ-omy to move from low inflation to deflation? What causes optimistic consumers to turn pessimistic? Clearly there must be a catalyst. In the 1920s, that catalyst was the crash of 1929 and the subsequent bear market, which wiped out almost 90 percent of the perceived "wealth" in stocks. I fear another such catalyst may loom on the horizon today.

CHAPTER

3

SPECULATION AND MANIAS

In December of 1996, with the Dow Jones Industrial Average at about 6,000, Fed Chairman Alan Greenspan used the term "irrational exuberance" to describe the American public's apparent infatuation with the stock market. In spite of this clear warning from the most powerful financial official in the world, many Americans continued to pour their savings into the most overvalued stock market of this century. By late 1998, the market had advanced another 50 percent, surpassing 9,000 on the Dow. No less that Warren Buffet and George Soros, arguably the two most successful and admired investors of this era, also have publicly aired their concerns about the market today. Still investors keep buying and the market keeps getting more expensive. Americans are indeed infatuated with the stock market.

Of all the signs of market excesses that have appeared in the last couple of years, none is more blatant or disturbing than America's willingness to ignore the comments of Greenspan, Soros and Buffett. These men are not just admired, they're idolized. Greenspan is widely credited on Wall Street for having successfully guided our economy through the crash of 1987 and for directing the longest post-war expansion on record. Soros and Buffet both have used their investment intelligence to amass fortunes on Wall Street. For a long time now, Soros has been "king" of the hedge fund investors. At the same time Buffett has been so successful buying (and holding) stocks that thousands of investors flock to his home town of Omaha, Nebraska, each year just to hear what Warren has to say at the annual Berkshire Hathaway meeting. What used to be a small gathering of investors is now a convention!

Individually, these men have enormous respect and clout. Collectively their influence on Wall Street should be overwhelming. It's the investment equivalent of having Michael Jordan, Larry Bird, and Magic Johnson on the same basketball team.

While these men have become celebrities, it's not because they're prone to make public their opinions of the financial markets. Indeed, their positions of power and influence dictate that they be evasive, almost secretive, when making comments about the financial markets. Yet, in spite of their well-known aversion to publicity, these men have chosen to publicly question the level of the market in the last few years. Why? Certainly, Greenspan, as head of the Federal Reserve, took a highly unusual step in raising the issue of "irrational exuberance." Fed chairmen by tradition don't raise controversial issues that might be misinterpreted by the general public. Greenspan, moreover, is a man who chooses his words very, very carefully. There's little doubt that his comments were intended to dampen speculation in the stock market.

While Buffett is certainly interested in financial gain, it's clearly not in his interest to "talk down" the market when he has billions invested in stocks. As for Soros, his intentions and interests are perhaps less clear to the average investor. After all, hedge funds can benefit from both the short and long side of the market. However, Soros has always emphasized his belief that markets naturally tend toward disequilibrium, swinging back and forth from overvaluation to undervaluation. Soros has consistently recommended that governments play a greater role in providing stability to the financial markets. Once again, these public comments are contrary to his financial interests since hedge funds thrive on volatility.[1]

Clearly, Buffet and Soros are not speaking with their wallets in mind. They are, I believe, speaking out of a sense of public duty. They recognize that we're in the midst of a speculative bubble that threatens the future of our market and our economy. In fact, Greenspan, in commenting on the "irrational exuberance" of today's market, specifically referred to the American market of the 1920s and Japan's market of the 1980s as examples of what can happen to the real economy when a stock market bubble bursts.

If these men are so influential, why has the market continued to rise in spite of their public warnings? Why are many average investors ignoring the most respected men on Wall Street? Are we indeed witnessing a mania (which, by definition, defies logic)? If we are, then the behavior of the average investor, though irrational, is understandable.

Is there any way to prove or disprove the existence of a mania? The simple answer is "no." Most of the signs of a mania are subjective. However, there's one sign of a stock market mania that's much more objective: extreme overvaluation. As the next chapter will illustrate, this market has entered a zone of overvaluation that has only two precedents in modern history, the American stock market of the late 1920s and Japan's bubble of the late 1980s. In both cases, the stock market collapsed, deflation set in, and the economy entered a severe

---

[1]Hedge funds allow their managers a great deal of investment flexibility, including margin purchases and short sales.

downturn. The obvious parallels between today's market and those prior periods could be a coincidence, but that probability is quite small. In fact, it requires a great leap of faith to rationalize the astronomical valuations in our market and ignore the potential consequences.

In spite of the clear risks that we face, most people scoff at the notion that our market could be as overpriced or risky as the market of the late 1920s. Most assume that the 1920s-1930s boom/bust period was a historical aberration that will never be repeated. But what do we know about speculation in the 1920s?

One fact many people acknowledge is that margin requirements at the time were only 10 percent. This means that a person who wanted to buy $1,000 worth of stock was required to deposit only $100 or 10 percent. Today the comparable margin requirement is $500—50 percent. This often leads to the simple conclusion that speculation in the 1920s was far greater than what we have today.

In reality, gauging the amount of speculation in a market is far more complex than simply looking at the margin requirements for retail investors. The nature and the methods of speculation have changed markedly over the years. We must look at all facets of speculation if we hope to understand it and quantify it. It's true that lower margin requirements generally encourage more speculation. All other things being equal, it's therefore reasonable to assume that the higher requirements today would lead to a "safer" market than we had in the 1920s. Unfortunately, all other things are not equal.

First, today the derivatives (futures and options) markets allow individuals and institutions to speculate with effective margin requirements well below 10 percent. Additionally, the size and global scope of the derivatives markets are truly unprecedented. Virtually every major financial institution in the world invests through highly leveraged derivatives every day. Of course, most of these positions are being hedged[2] to prevent losses from getting out of control in rapidly moving markets. In reality, though, there's little reason to be optimistic that all the hedges will perform as expected. On the contrary, there's much evidence from the last decade to suggest that hedges are *not* perfect, occasionally increasing risk rather than mitigating it.

The demise of the hedge fund Long-Term Capital in 1998 amply illustrates my point. This fund was employing leverage in excess of 30 to 1. Its managers assumed that the risks inherent in that amount of leverage were offset by the hedges they had in place. However, when markets moved in an unanticipated direction, the hedges proved useless. Losses spiraled out of control, bringing global financial markets to the breaking point. In our increasingly leveraged world of global finance, it's highly likely that we'll experience more of these "financial accidents" that threaten our economic well being.

In the final analysis, speculation is determined by the total amount of leverage employed by all investors and consumers. In this light, the speculation in today's economy dwarfs anything we have ever seen.

Another factor that distinguishes our market from the 1920s is the degree of public participation. While we've all heard stories about shoeshine boys giving stock tips to bankers in the 1920s, the reality was that the market then was a game for the wealthy. Today, however, stock ownership is far more widespread. It's interesting that the public, by and large, seems to take comfort in this fact; having lots of company makes investors feel more secure. With so many other stock investors, many feel the market is more solid and predictable! But where's the logic to this line of reasoning? The reality is that the broad public participation that helps fuel the mania while the market is rising will inevitably accentuate the decline when confidence begins to erode.

---

[2]Hedging is a practice that seeks to insure that certain risks in one security are offset by gains in another.

The broad participation in today's market is due in large part to the dramatic growth of mutual funds and 401k retirement accounts. Indeed the growth has been explosive: Since 1987, the number of mutual funds has grown from 431 to well over 10,000. In general, mutual funds have been a blessing to the average retail investor. Funds traditionally have much lower transaction costs in comparison to individual investing. Additionally, funds have greater diversification, which presumably lowers risk. However, just as the risk reduction provided by hedges is sometimes an illusion, the assumed safety of mutual funds may be misleading. The public's current love affair with mutual funds (see Figure 3-1) may inadvertently fuel speculation, thereby increasing risk.

Figure 3-1 Mutual Fund Assets

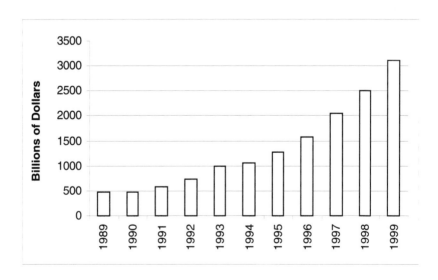

Source: Federal Reserve Statistics

How can this happen? As the average investor gains confidence in the positive attributes of mutual funds, it's rational to assume that investors will allocate more of their financial assets to funds than they would otherwise allocate to individual stocks. As long as mutual funds continue to provide good returns, this trend can be expected to continue. For a while, it may even be a self-fulfilling prophecy: As mutual funds receive more cash, they buy more stock, causing greater demand and higher stock prices. This cycle leads to good fund performance, which attracts even more cash. Ultimately this phenomenon will lead to a severe overvaluation. This seems to be exactly what's happening today.

Why do fund managers continue buying when stocks have become overvalued? First, managers often have no choice but to invest the money they receive. Most funds are required by prospectus to invest a minimum percentage (often 40 to 95 percent) of their assets in the stock market. In fact, many of the largest funds today are index funds, which must always be fully invested in stocks.

Additionally, we shouldn't forget that mutual fund managers are human beings. Like the rest of us, they can be swept up in the euphoria of a bull market. This is especially true for the relatively young fund manager who hasn't experienced a full-fledged bear market. Unfortunately 80 percent of today's mutual fund managers were in high school during the 1987 crash; many were still in diapers during the last true bear market of 1973-1974.

To fully understand why managers buy highly priced stocks, we must realize that the fund management business is extremely competitive. Since the bull market began in 1982, the stock market has risen almost 19 percent a year. In the last five years, the growth rate has accelerated to well over 20 percent a year. In this environment, fund managers can ill afford to sit in cash if they hope to stay competitive. Managers who sit on cash waiting for a correction are doomed to under-performance.

Several years ago Jeffrey Vinik, manager of the Fidelity Magellan Fund, decided to make a temporary bet on bonds in his portfolio. His timing was a bit off, causing the fund to underperform the stock market. Shortly thereafter, he found himself out of a job, even though he had a very fine long-term track record. The moral of this story was not lost on other managers. Ever since, very few managers have tried to time the market. Today, most managers accept the fact that they must be fully invested in stocks if they want to keep their jobs.

But being fully invested is only part of the challenge facing fund managers today. For the last couple of years the market has been led by a small group of very expensive stocks, primarily in the technology sector. Fund managers who choose to avoid these stocks because they're wary of the high valuations are punished with severe under-performance. On the other hand, managers who ignore the inherent risks in these expensive stocks, and overweight them in their portfolios are rewarded with strong performance. The result is that tech-heavy funds are dramatically outperforming the market, attracting even more money to the technology sector. Of course, this phenomenon won't last forever. Eventually the technology bubble will burst and investors will once again come to respect valuations and risks. But in the meantime the pressure on managers to stay fully invested, and to be in technology stocks, is enormous.

The growth of the 401k defined contribution retirement plan market has been comparable to the dramatic growth in mutual funds (see Figure 3-2). The employee funds most of the contributions to 401k plans; traditional defined benefit plans require the corporation to fund the entire contribution. In short, a 401k is much less costly for an employer to operate than a traditional pension plan. Over the past decade, more and more corporations have decided to convert their defined benefit retirement plans to defined contribution plans (the most important of which is the 401k). Today these assets exceed $2.5 trillion dollars. According to recent surveys, approximately 70 percent of these assets are invested in the stock market.[3]

Figure 3-2 Pension Plans Asset Growth (Net Acquisition of Financial Assets)

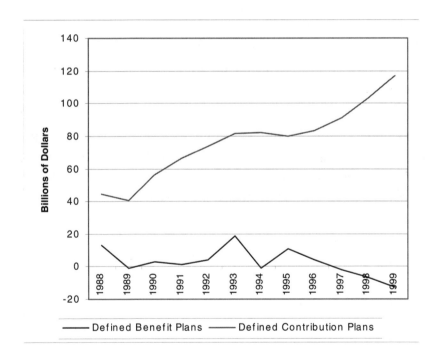

Source: Federal Reserve Statistics

---

[3]"A Nation of Millionaires," *Barron's*, March 27, 2000.

On the surface, the tremendous growth in 401ks seems to be a clear positive for working-class Americans. It's no secret that the average American needs additional retirement savings to supplement social security income. However, in many cases the 401k is an *alternative* retirement plan rather than an *additional* one.

The difference between a traditional pension plan and a 401k is enormous. In traditional pension plans employees are promised a fixed benefit at retirement. The pension plan assets are managed by professional investment advisors. Employees are generally unaware of how plan assets are allocated; they are detached from the emotional gyrations of the stock market. They're likely to feel secure about their retirement regardless of what the market does in any given month or year.

With 401k-type retirement plans, employees make their own asset allocation decisions. Often these assets represent the largest component of the employees' net worth. Employees realize that their investment decisions and the performance of the stock market can have a major impact on their retirement. This system places an enormous responsibility on employees. Unfortunately, most employees are not sophisticated investors and are uncomfortable with this responsibility.

What are the implications of this change for the market and the economy?

What we have done as a society is to move a tremendous pool of savings away from professional investment advisors into the hands of immature investors. There are exceptions, of course. Some employees have the tools and the inclination to become astute investors. But most employees are inexperienced; they can be expected to behave more emotionally than a professional money manager. Furthermore, they generally lack the skills to evaluate the overall risk in the market as well as the risks in the real economy. When the next bear market arrives, these employees are likely to react the way most immature investors react: They'll become nervous as the market begins to decline and they'll sell as they begin to lose faith in the market's ability to rebound.

Optimists may tell you that investors have learned since the crash of 1987 to buy stocks on declines, rather than sell. Indeed, "buying the dips" is a strategy that's worked marvelously throughout this extraordinary bull market. Each decline in the market has been quickly followed by new highs. Time and time again, investors buying the dips have been rewarded with quick profits.

This will change. There will soon come a time when the dips aren't promptly followed by new highs. Investors won't get the immediate gratification to which they've become accustomed. Eventually, investors buying the dips will be punished with quick losses.

As the reality of this sets in, the psychology—and the behavior—of the inexperienced investor will change. Ultimately, when the market is near its low, these investors will become so disillusioned with the market that they will sell. The fear and the pain will simply be too much to bear.

Some will criticize this pessimistic analysis as extreme. However, there's nothing radical about this potential scenario. In fact, this pattern has been typical of investors throughout history. The different and disturbing aspect about today's environment is that so many inexperienced investors are responsible for the safety of their retirement nest egg.

While all this is troubling enough, there's an additional factor to consider. Our economy today is saddled with huge amounts of personal debt. Credit card and home equity loans have risen to levels that would have been unthinkable in prior eras. During the next recession, the combination of a weak economy and a sinking stock market will make the average employee very nervous about retirement. As this employee watches his or her primary asset (the 401k) decline in value, personal debt will seem increasingly burdensome. As a result, employees and investors will become even more emotional as they try to make investment decisions. This scenario increases the probability that they'll sell into weakness.

It's not just 401ks that we have to worry about. Over the last seven or eight years, ordinary middle-class Americans have flocked to no-load mutual funds, deep-discount brokers, and Internet stock trading. These investors have been moving away from the traditional broker relationship, attracted by lower commissions and their tremendous access to information via the Internet.

When the next prolonged bear market arrives, it will be the first time in history that a large portion of the investing public has no bro-ker or investment advisor to provide guidance during an extended stock market decline. Many of these investors have been lured into the do-it-yourself approach with unrealistic expectations. The long bull market has led many unsuspecting investors to believe that the stock market is a one-way street heading uphill. Some recent surveys indi-cate these investors are expecting long-term returns averaging 20 to 30 percent a year. Clearly, these newcomers are extrapolating returns from the recent past, ignoring the reality of history, which indicates stock market returns in the 10 to12 percent zone.

They're in for a rude awakening. The next bear market will teach them two things: (1) returns of 20 to 30 percent over the long run are not realistic; (2) even more modest returns of 10 to 12 percent are achieved only by subjecting oneself to hefty doses of market volatili-ty. Many will find this volatility overwhelming and unacceptable. They'll relieve their discomfort by selling.

Of course, it's not just the do-it-yourselfers who have unrealistic expectations these days. The long bull market has influenced the expectations and the behavior of the majority of investors. But the broad public participation that has propelled this market to dizzying heights will reverse course as the next bear market brings expectations back to reality. The public will become a source of relentless selling, eventually bringing the market back to a state of significant undervaluation. As you'll see in the next chapter, that process is likely to be long and painful.

4

OVERVALUATION

Excessive optimism leads to excessive speculation, which ultimately leads to extreme valuation. The evidence of overvaluation today is not just compelling it's overwhelming.

Analysts use a variety of statistics to judge a market's valuation. Most of these statistics compare the current price of the market to other variables, such as earnings, cash flow, dividends, book value, sales and even gross domestic product (GDP). While no single statistic can be relied on consistently and accurately to judge the market, by looking at many financial ratios we can see whether a market has become cheap or expensive.

Valuation measures aren't used to determine when and what will cause an overvalued market to turn down or an undervalued market to turn up. In other words, they aren't timing tools. Nonetheless, it's crucial for long-term investors to understand that valuation tools are the only rational means of estimating potential risks and rewards.

In today's market, most optimists support their bullish stance by focusing on price/earnings (P/E) ratios, which compares a stock price to the company's earnings per share. This ratio, which can be used on an individual stock or on the market as a whole, is probably the best known and most widely quoted statistic today. Simply speaking, higher P/Es imply more expensive markets; lower P/Es indicate cheaper markets. Normally, P/E ratios are compared to current interest rates to decide whether valuations are cheap, expensive, or average. This makes sense because stocks compete with other investments, like bonds, for the investor dollar. As interest rates move lower, investors are willing to pay more for earnings, so P/E ratios rise. Conversely, as rates move higher, investors are willing to pay less for earnings, so P/E ratios decline.

Over the past century, P/E ratios have fluctuated between lows of 6 to 7 times earnings when stocks are unpopular to highs of 20 to 25 times earnings when stocks are popular and interest rates low. While the inverse relationship between interest rates and P/E ratios has generally held true over this period, there have been times when the two seemed unrelated. For instance, in the late 1940s and early 1950s, though interest rates were very low (2.5 percent to 3.25 percent), P/E ratios stayed modest (7 to 12) because people remained wary of stocks after the Depression of the 1930s and the war years of the 1940s.

In addition, the P/E ratio itself can be very misleading because earnings can fluctuate greatly year to year. In 1930-1933, the P/E of the S&P index rose dramatically even as the market fell (see Figure 4-1). However, the P/E ratio was elevated not because the market (P) was expensive but because during the Depression corporate earnings (E) virtually disappeared. It was one of the best times in history to accumulate stocks, yet anyone strictly focused on the P/E ratio would have been reluctant to buy them because the P/E ratio looked expensive.

Paradoxically, in 1928-1929 the P/E ratio (14 to15) looked reasonable because interest rates were low (4 to 5 percent) and earnings growth was healthy. As we now know, this was one of the highest risk periods of the century. Investors who bought stocks during this period were virtually wiped out over the next three years and had to wait almost 25 years to recover their losses.

Figure 4-1 S&P Composite P/E Ratio

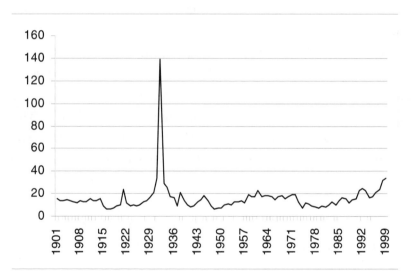

Source: Global Financial Data

Obviously, the P/E ratio leaves much to be desired as a valuation tool. Looking at Figure 4-1, you could be excused for thinking that stocks should be bought when P/Es are high and sold when P/Es are low! But equally clearly, the P/E ratio can be valuable used in conjunction with other valuation measures and in the context of prevailing interest rates. However, by itself, the P/E ratio gives off a lot of false signals of market risk.

In spite of this, the P/E ratio concept continues to be widely quoted. Why? I suspect the primary appeal of the P/E ratio is that it's a concept the general public can readily understand. It's quite logical that the price of a stock should be related to its earnings. Unfortunately, one of the main shortcomings of the P/E ratio is that earnings can fluctuate considerably from year to year. Also some analysts use overly optimistic assumptions about future earnings to justify current stock prices. Thus, the P/E ratio is more subject to abuse than other valuation tools.

For example, Figure 4-1 shows that the S&P index is now trading at over 30 times earnings—the highest P/E ratio ever recorded during a period of economic growth. While this should make investors cautious, bullish advisors are likely to minimize its significance. They may claim that we're in a new era of non-inflationary growth with continued low interest rates, and that justifies higher P/E ratios. Or they may assert that earnings are set to explode over the next several years, implying that the current P/E ratio is very modest based on future earnings. With some optimistic assumptions about interest rates and earnings, a bullish analyst might convince you that today's sky-high P/E ratios are actually cheap.

This line of thinking may seem reasonable to the casual observer. However, if we look a little deeper we quickly see that the P/E ratio is even higher that it appears. Many of today's large capitalization stocks do not trade on the New York Stock Exchange, as they did in the 1920s or in the 1960s. These companies, like Microsoft and Intel, trade over the counter on the NASDAQ market,[1] where many of

---

[1] Intel and Microsoft were added to the Dow Industrial Averages on November 1, 1999.

today's most popular stocks trade, including heavyweights in technology as well as rising stars of the Internet. Clearly we need to include some of these large stocks if we want an accurate comparison with the P/E ratios of prior periods. While some of these issues are included in the S&P index, many aren't, which means that the Dow and S&P averages actually underestimate current P/E ratios. At the market peak, in mid-1998, the NASDAQ average was trading at an astounding 70 times earnings (see Figure 4-2). This is comparable to the P/E ratio we saw in Japan in the late 1980s, just as its bubble was about to burst.

Figure 4-2 NASDAQ Composite Index

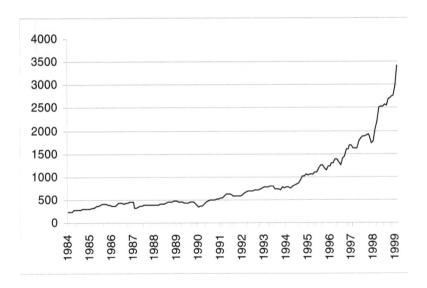

Source: Economagic.com

The NASDAQ did not come into existence until 1971 and did not really become an economic force until the 1980s. It was then that the technology-dominated NASDAQ index began to gain notoriety. While we can't compare the P/E ratios of today's NASDAQ market with those of prior bull markets, we clearly can no longer afford to ignore this market index. According to Bianco Research,[2] the capitalization of the NASDAQ market surpassed $6.5 trillion by March of 2000, up 150 percent from the beginning of 1999. At this rate of growth, the NASDAQ could surpass the market capitalization of the NYSE ($10.2 trillion) within a year. As you'll see later in this chapter, these statistics are incredible when you consider that the entire output of the U.S. economy amounts to "only" $9.5 trillion. Even more amazing is the fact that the P/E ratio of the NASDAQ index continues to rise dramatically as more and more Internet IPOs (with little or no earnings) are added to the index. By March of 2000, the NASDAQ had reached an incredible P/E ratio of 200 times earnings!

While analysts may debate which indexes to use for comparison, there's no question that overall P/E ratios today are much higher than ever before.

Another reason that the market P/E ratio is nevertheless understated is that current earnings are clearly overstated, due to two factors:

1. The use of stock options to compensate employees has grown dramatically over this bull market. This practice of using options rather than cash as compensation lowers reported costs and raises reported earnings. One recent study indicates that profits would have been 50 percent lower in 1998 if option costs had been expensed correctly. That means the average P/E ratio on the S&P would have been 63 at year-end 1998.[3]

---

[2]*Barron's*, March 13, 2000, "Tortoise And Hare," pg 19.
[3]*Barron's*, April 12, 1999 "Upand Down Wall St."

2. "Nonrecurring costs" are excluded from earnings on corporate income statements. The problem is that many of the supposedly nonrecurring costs end up recurring. The fact that corporate America is going through a period of almost constant restructuring makes it very difficult to discern what the true level of earnings should be for many large corporations. The endless daily mergers, acquisitions, layoffs, and spin-offs give corporations numerous opportunities to record "nonrecurring" charges. I'm not suggesting that all companies that take nonrecurring charges are trying to hide their real earnings. After all, higher nonrecurring charges are to be expected during a period of rapid consolidation; such as we're currently experiencing. Nonetheless, most corporations will try to post the highest earnings allowable under current accounting rules.

While the issue of real versus reported earnings is not a new one, the size and importance of the problem are new. Corporations today are under enormous pressure to produce consistent earnings growth. Why? Because consistent-growth companies today are rewarded with very high P/E ratios relative to more erratic stocks. For instance, at the end of 1998 Coca Cola was trading at a P/E ratio of 45, even though earnings growth had slowed to under 10 percent a year. Coke was given a high P/E multiple because it's perceived as a consistent growth stock.

A high P/E ratio translates into a high stock price, which can be an enormous advantage. A high stock price can lower a corporation's cost of capital (the company can sell shares to retire high-cost debt) or to acquire another company that trades at a much lower P/E ratio. It's no coincidence that most of today's mergers and acquisitions involve the exchange not of cash but of stock. A high P/E ratio, in essence, has become a new, very valuable, currency.

The result of all this is that corporate management today has a tremendous incentive to produce consistent earnings growth. The combination of generous stock options and very high P/E ratios can lead to the creation of enormous wealth for senior management. Certainly, Bill Gates is a prime example of what consistent earnings growth and a high P/E will do for your net worth.

In the euphoria of a raging bull market, most investors will overlook mundane issues such as the accounting treatment of nonrecurring costs. But when this bull market ends investors will take a closer look at reported earnings. When they do, they will find that reported earnings are quite often higher than real earnings. In the meantime, investors would be wise to cast a suspicious eye on corporations whose quarterly earnings always seem to contain nonrecurring charges.

As we have just seen, the problem with using the P/E ratio as a valuation tool is that earnings fluctuate too much and are often simply unreliable. Consequently, analysts use many valuation techniques in addition to the P/E.

One of the most reliable indicators over the years has been the price/dividend ratio, which tells us how much investors are willing to pay for a dollar of stock dividends. Over the past 100 years, investors have generally paid between 15 and 30 times dividends for stocks (see Figure 4-3). Every time the Dow approached or exceeded 30 times dividends—see 1929, 1965,1972, and 1987—the market suffered a major setback. Conversely, every time the market fell to or below 15 times dividends—see 1932, 1942, 1949, and 1982—the market has hit a major bottom.

Figure 4-3 Dow Jones Price Dividend Ratio

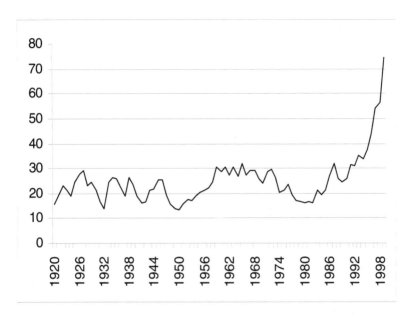

Source: Value Line

By the first quarter of 2000, the Dow was trading at 70 times dividends, while the S&P 500 was over 80 times dividends. Only in a mania of monstrous proportions could investors rationalize this behavior.

Critics will argue that this indicator is no longer valid because corporations are choosing to use cash flow to buy back stock rather than to increase dividends. Indeed large corporate buybacks have increased dramatically since 1991, rising from about $25 billion a year to about $150 Billion a year by 1998. However, even if that cash flow had been used to increase dividends, the market would still be vastly overvalued. As you can see from figures 4-4, 4-5, and 4-6 dividends have

Figure 4-4 Stock Dividend Growth

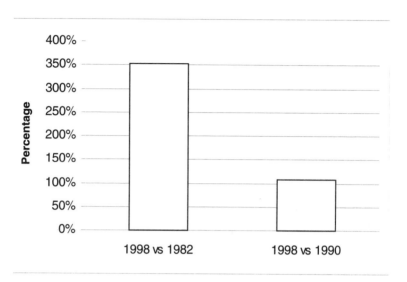

Figure 4-5 Corporate Net Cash Flow Growth

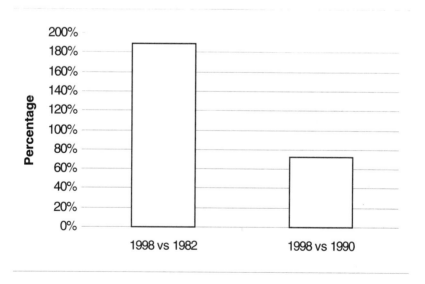

Source: Economagic.com

actually grown faster than cash flow during the course of this bull market. Yet, amongst the largest U.S. corporations, dividend growth has not kept pace with earnings growth (see Figure 4-7). SP 500 earnings grew noticeably faster than S&P 500 dividends between 1982 and 1998. This anomaly is very likely due to the growing tendency of large corporations to repurchase stock rather than increase dividends. (This phenomenon may also explain why large stocks have vastly outperformed small stocks during the 1990s).

Figure 4-6 S&P 500 Dividend vs. Share Buybacks

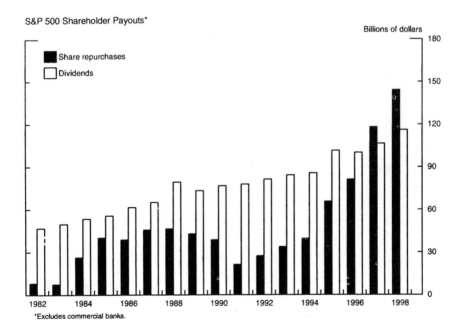

S&P 500 Shareholder Payouts*

■ Share repurchases
☐ Dividends

Billions of dollars

*Excludes commercial banks.

Source: Compustat

If we were to make the reasonable assumption that dividends should have increased in line with earnings during this period, then we would arrive at current S&P dividends of 22 to 23 (versus 16) and a price/dividend ratio of approximately 60 times dividends. This "adjusted" ratio is still far above all prior bull market peak levels. Given the tremendous track record of this indicator, one can only assume that this market is in big trouble once this mania has ended. In the meantime, it's rather ironic that bullish analysts would like us to take comfort in the knowledge that many corporations are using cash to buy stocks.

Figure 4-7 S&P 500 Earnings and Dividend Growth

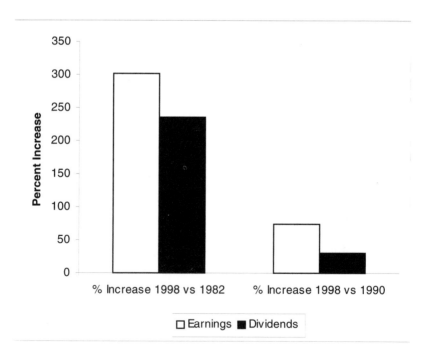

Source: S&P Statistics (Analysts Handbook)

IBM (see Figure 4-8) is a good example of a corporation that has chosen in recent years to use cash flow to aggressively repurchase stock rather than increase dividends. Over the four-year period from December 31, 1994, through December 31, 1998, IBM used cash to reduce stock outstanding by 250 million shares. In other words, IBM repurchased over 20 percent of its stock in four years. The cost of this was about $27 billion. At the same time, the company spent only about $3 billion on dividend payments. So, IBM spent almost ten times as much money repurchasing stock as it did paying dividends!

Figure 4-8 IBM Financials 1994 through 1998

Annual Balance Sheet

Fiscal Year End	12/31/98	12/31/97	12/31/96	12/31/95	12/31/94
Assets					
Cash & Equivalents	5,768.00	7,553.00	8,137.00	7,701.00	10,554.00
Total Current Assets	42,360.00	40,418.00	40,695.00	40,691.00	41,338.00
Total Assets	86,100.00	81,499.00	81,132.00	80,292.00	81,091.00
Liabilities & Shareholder's Equity					
Total Current Liabilities	36,827.00	33,507.00	34,000.00	31,648.00	29,226.00
Long Term Debt	15,508.00	13,696.00	9,872.00	10,060.00	12,548.00
Total Liabilities	66,667.00	61,683.00	59,504.00	57,869.00	57,678.00
Total Shareholder's Equity	19,433.00	19,816.00	21,628.00	22,423.00	23,413.00
Average Shares Outstanding	925.1	968.48	1,016.80	1,094.80	1,175.00
Book Value a Share	20.79	20.12	20.48	19.85	19.11

Annual Income Statement (in millions except EPS data)

Fiscal Year End	12/31/98	12/31/97	12/31/96	12/31/95	12/31/94
Sales	81,667.00	78,508.00	75,947.00	71,940.00	64,052.00
Net Income	6,328.00	6,093.00	5,429.00	4,178.00	3,021.00
Earnings a Share Data					
Average Shares	960.1	1,010.48	1,056.80	1,167.80	1,170.00
Diluted Net EPS	6.57	6.01	5.12	3.53	2.51
Dividends a Share	0.88	0.78	0.65	0.5	0.5
Total Dividends Paid	844	787	686	583	585

Source: Zack's Investment Research and Value Line

As you can see from Figure 4-9, IBM shareholders were amply rewarded during this period, however, as the stock rose from under $20 a share to almost $100 a share, a rise of over 500 percent. At first glance, one might assume that IBM has been a wonderful example of a stodgy old technology firm reinventing itself into a dynamic growth company of the 1990s. One might also be tempted to assume that IBM has wisely used cash flow to repurchase stock, thereby maximizing its value to shareholders.

Figure 4-9 IBM Stock Price Charted

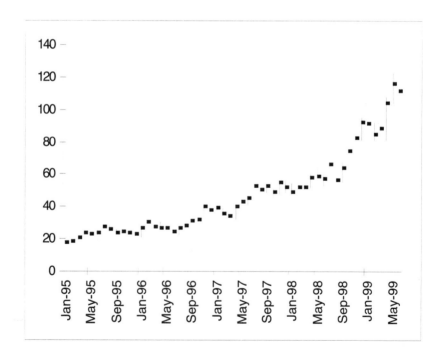

Source: CSI Inc.

But is this view justified? On further reflection, a different and less bullish picture emerges. Over this four-year period, IBM's total revenues increased from $64 billion to $82 billion, or just over 28 percent. Cash flow increased from $9.1 billion to $11.2 billion (23 percent) and earnings increased from $3.0 billion to $6.3 billion (113 percent). At the same time, IBM's book value declined from $23 billion to $19 billion; working capital[5] declined from $12 billion to $5.5 billion; cash declined from $10 billion to $5 billion. Meanwhile, IBM's long-term debt increased from $12.5 billion to $15.5 billion.

What do all these numbers indicate? In these four years, IBM grew revenues modestly and cut costs, more than doubling earnings. However, what is most striking is that IBM dramatically reduced its liquidity (measured by working capital[5]) and equity base (measured by book value). At the same time, the company has aggressively used its free cash flow to repurchase stock at progressively higher prices. Over the period IBM's P/E ratio has increased from 15 times earnings to 29 times earnings.

Did IBM use its cash prudently, in a way that will benefit long-term shareholders? Only history will give us a definite answer. In the meantime, IBM has clearly become a more leveraged company. The additional leverage (debt) implies less financial flexibility. Will this create a problem for IBM during the next economic downturn? If it does, investors in IBM will look back on this period of aggressive stock repurchases with regret. They will realize that using cash to purchase high-priced stock may provide a good return to short-term speculators but it's detrimental to long-term investors.

The questions raised by this example are by no means unique to IBM. In many ways IBM is typical of what has been taking place recently in the U.S. economy and the U.S stock market: Stock prices

---

[5]Working capital is current assets (including cash) less current liabilities.

have risen far more rapidly than sales and earnings. The questions and conclusions that arise from the IBM analysis are equally relevant to the market as a whole.

I am not suggesting that IBM has willfully inflated its stock price. I do believe it has engaged in a bit of "irrational exuberance."

I also don't want to imply that there is anything wrong with stock buybacks per se. For corporations with excess cash flow and cheap stock prices, buybacks may indeed be prudent and beneficial to long-term shareholders. However, since stock buybacks have mushroomed while valuations have skyrocketed, it seems logical to question the sanity of buybacks.

Tremendous bull markets have a way of attracting demand from traditionally conservative entities. In the 1920s, many banks were guilty of playing the stock market with depositors' money. Today huge amounts of corporate cash flow is being used to purchase stock, often at very high P/E ratios. In more conservative times, this cash flow would be used to retire debt or retained to strengthen the balance sheet. If we're indeed witnessing a stock market bubble, then history may well judge today's corporate stock repurchases much as we judged bank activities in the 1920s: Corporations will be viewed as having participated in an activity that was outside their corporate charter—stock speculation.

Another valuation tool that has been useful over the years is the price/book value ratio. While this indicator doesn't have as good a track record as the price/dividend ratio, it has nonetheless been accurate in identifying periods of extreme under- or over-valuation. Since 1920 the price/book ratio of the Dow has generally fluctuated between one times book at market lows to a little under two times book at market highs (see Figure 4-10). Before 1990, the only times the market significantly exceeded that peak were in 1987, when the ratio reached 2.75, and 1929, when the ratio exceeded 4. Obviously those were both important market tops. Conversely, whenever the Dow fell below one times book (1982, 1974, 1942 and 1932), the market made a major low.

Figure 4-10 Dow Jones Price/Book Ratio

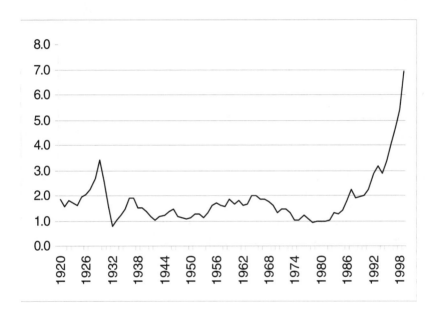

Source: Value Line

Yet, since 1991 the Dow has consistently traded above two times book, yet the market has risen. By April 2000, this ratio had risen to almost seven.

How can we explain this? Once again accounting adjustments have distorted the ratio. Since 1990, American corporations have undertaken a massive restructuring in a largely successful effort to become more efficient and competitive. This restructuring led to the write-down of major assets, resulting in lower book values for many companies. From 1990 through 1995, the book value of the Dow failed to rise in spite of steady growth in the economy. This is highly unusual and is clearly due to restructuring charges. However, even if we make some optimistic assumptions about book values today, the market is still grossly overvalued.

It took from 1953 to 1968—15 years—for the book value of the Dow to double. This was a period of very rapid growth for the U.S. economy. It took from 1968 to 1988—20 years—for Dow book value to double again. Even if we were to make the incredibly optimistic assumption that the real book value of the Dow has doubled since 1988 (only 12 years), we would arrive at an adjusted book value of 2,150 in 2000 vs. stated book value of 1,691. This means that at the recent Dow peak of 11,000, the market was trading at well over 5 times assumed book value, significantly higher than the previous high, in 1929.

While bullish analysts will try to tell you that the price/book and price/dividend ratios are no longer valid, the evidence clearly shows that even with very optimistic accounting adjustments, this is the most expensive market in history. Unfortunately for the bulls, the evidence against them does not stop there.

Another statistic used to gauge market valuation compares the value of all publicly traded stocks to U.S. GDP. From the 1920s until 1995, this ratio (stock value/GDP) has fluctuated between 30 and 80 percent (see Figure 4-11). A ratio that drops towards the 30 percent level indicates that stock prices are inexpensive relative to the nation's output of goods and services. This occurred in 1932-1933, 1942-1943, 1949, and 1974. All of these points were at or very close to major market bottoms. Conversely, when this ratio approached 80 percent, as it did in the late 1920s and the mid- to late 1960s, it indicated that the market was very expensive and near an important top.

Figure 4-11 Market Capitalization (NYSE, AMEX, NASDAQ)/GDP

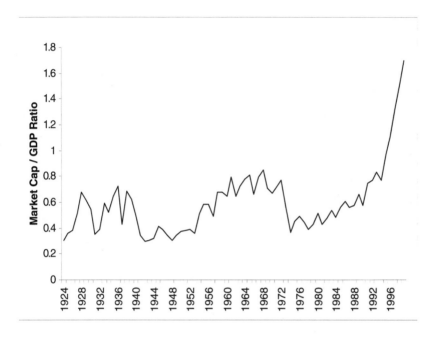

Source: Global Financial Data

Of course, this ratio can be distorted somewhat over time, as more companies may choose to go public when prices are high and fewer when prices are low. Nonetheless, this ratio has been a good indicator of market valuations (and risk) for almost 75 years.

Since 1995, this ratio has skyrocketed, along with the market. In 1998 it reached 160 percent. This is almost double the values we saw at previous bull market peaks. Once again we have a reliable indicator telling us that we're witnessing the most overvalued, and most risky, stock market of the century.

A similar valuation tool, the price/sales ratio compares the stock price to the underlying sales of the corporation (or the market). This valuation tool has distinct advantages over the other indicators: (1) it's not affected by the number of companies going public; and (2) sales are far less subject to manipulation and interpretation than book value or dividends. Therefore, this ratio is certainly useful for comparing today's market to prior periods.

During this century the S&P has traded between 40 percent of sales at market lows to 130 percent of sales at market highs. The previous peaks for this ratio occurred in 1929, just before the market crashed, and in the mid-1960s as the Dow approached 1,000. Both of these points represented important market tops that would not be overcome for more than a decade.

Figure 4-12 Standard & Poor's Industrial Average Price/Sales Ratio

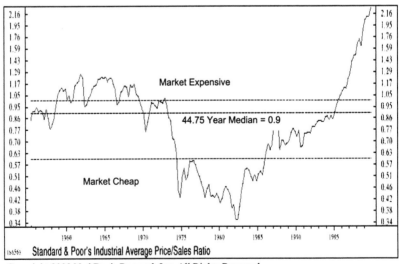

Over the last three years, this ratio has soared past all prior peaks to reach an incredible 200 percent of sales (see Figure 4-12). Keep in mind that the S&P index doesn't include most of the Internet stocks, which have incredibly high price/sales ratios. Today, the average Internet stock has a price/sales ratio of over 2,000 percent or 20 times! If we were to include all the NASDAQ stocks in this analysis, today's overvaluation would appear that much more extreme.

One final ratio that confirms the current overvaluation compares stock prices to personal income or wages. This valuation tool looks at how long it takes an average employee to earn wages to buy a share of the Dow. The longer it takes, the more expensive the market.

This ratio has been an excellent barometer of value over the past 50 years (see Figure 4-13). At the valuation peak in the mid-1960s, this ratio peaked at just under 40. Conversely, at the market bottom in 1982 it fell to almost 10.

By early 1999, with the Dow above 10,000, this ratio was approaching 80—twice the valuation peak of the mid-960s.

All these valuation tools have accurately pinpointed periods of extreme market overvaluation and undervaluation during this century. They all clearly indicate that today's market is the most expensive ever.

Could it simply be a coincidence that all these indicators are telling us the same thing? The odds of that are very small indeed. The only reasonable conclusion is that the market today has reached a valuation well beyond the previous high water mark of the century—1929.

Could these incredible valuations somehow be justified? The only rational justification for today's valuations would be the expectation that the U.S. economy is on the verge of a very long period of explosive, uninterrupted growth. Once again, the odds of this are extremely low.

Figure 4-13 Dow Jones Price vs Personal Income
            Index of Hourly Manufacturing Earnings

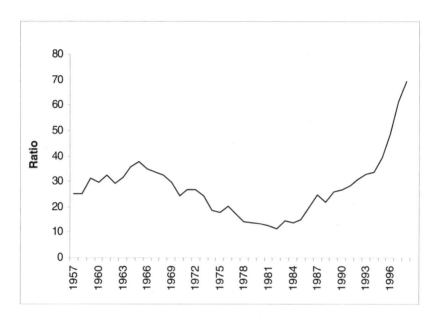

Source: Global Financial Data

These simple but obvious observations are difficult for most people to accept. Nobody wants to believe that we're part of a speculative orgy like that of 1929. The implications are unsettling: Most of us realize that speculative bubbles are often followed by great economic hardship. Uncertain about what lies ahead, most people choose, consciously or unconsciously, to remain optimistic about the future. Unfortunately, that optimism today seems dangerously out of synch with reality.

Valuation tools tell us if the market is cheap or expensive, but they do not tell us when the market will move up or down. However, the history of financial markets makes one point very clear: Periods of extreme market overvaluation are inevitably followed by severe bear markets that bring prices back to rational levels. Typically, the more excessive the overvaluation, the more severe the bear market. It's no coincidence that the most overvalued market of the century (1929) was followed by the most severe bear market (down 90 percent).

This huge decline led to the most undervalued market of this century (1932). What can we expect from the next bear market in the U.S.?

The valuation tools we've discussed clearly indicate that today's market is far more expensive that the market of the late 1960s and early 1970s, and apparently even more expensive than the 1929 market. Accordingly, we should expect a bear market significantly worse than what we experienced in 1973-1974 (down 45 percent). At the bottom in 1974, the Dow was trading at 77 percent of book value, 15 times dividends, and about 6 times earnings. Today those same valuations would imply a Dow average of between 1,500 and 2,500.

In 1932, the market bottomed at under 10 times dividends and 50 percent of book value. There were no earnings in 1932 due to the severity of the depression. An equivalent valuation today would put the Dow well below 1,500.

These numbers may seem unbelievable to the average investor today, but they are completely rational in the context of market history. What's truly unbelievable today is the complacency of investors in the face of enormous risks.

Chapter

5

Debt and Savings

An excessively valued stock market, in and of itself, is cause for concern. The process of deflating an overvalued market can destroy a large amount of wealth, which inevitably must have a strong negative impact on the real economy. To fully understand the risk we face today, we need to examine the potential effect of a deflating market in the context of a highly leveraged, consumer driven economy. It's precisely this combination of an extremely overvalued market and an overextended consumer that puts us in a very precarious situation.

America's dependence on the stock market has never been greater (see Figure 5-1). Since this bull market began in 1982, the stock market's share of household wealth has grown from under 10 percent to over 35 percent, surpassing the previous highs of the late sixties.

Figure 5-1 Equity Holdings/Household Net Worth

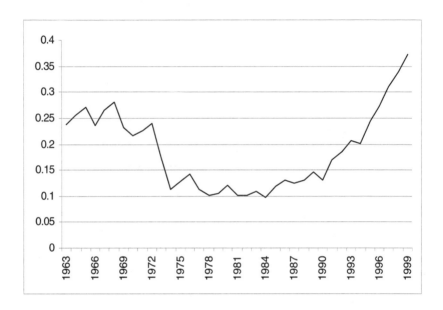

Source: Federal Reserve Statistics

If America had very high personal savings, then the value of stock holdings would be less of a concern. But the savings rate in America has dropped steadily since the early 1980s; it now stands at an all-time low of virtually zero (see Figure 5-2). Optimists will argue that the savings rate is no longer valid because it doesn't include money put into stock mutual funds, an increasingly common practice for American households. Should we consider the stock market as a form of savings, like certificates of deposit or money market funds? The logical answer is that we probably should count some of the money going into stocks as savings, perhaps 50 percent, but not all.

Figure 5-2 Personal Savings Rate

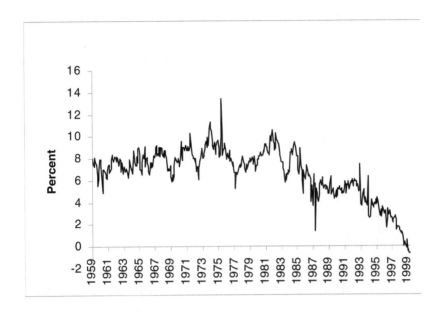

Source: Economagic.com

For the moment let's accept the bullish case, which argues that the real savings rate today is closer to 2 or 2.5 percent when adjusted for money going into stocks. Yet even this adjusted savings rate is still far below that of the mid- to late sixties, the last time the American consumer had so much riding on the stock market.

Further evidence of the vulnerability of the American consumer is provided in Figure 5-3. As you can see, the liquidity of the average American has been in a steady decline since this bull market began in the early 1980s. Consumers continue to take on debt at a rate that exceeds the growth of liquid assets, which include savings accounts, money market funds, and Treasury bills. As a result, the traditional safety net provided by liquid assets is gradually disappearing. More than ever before, Americans are betting on the stock market to satisfy current financial needs and reach long-term financial goals.

Figure 5-3 Household Liquidity

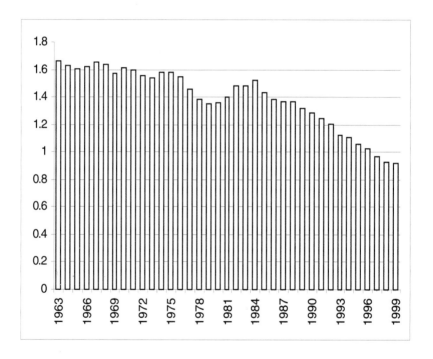

Source: Federal Reserve Board Flow of Funds

Clearly, a severe bear market today would have a dramatic effect on the financial health of the American consumer. Would this alone cause consumers to slow spending, bringing on a recession?

The interaction between the stock market and the economy is complex. At times a falling market (1929) seems to weaken the economy. At other times a falling market (1987) seems to have little impact on the economy. While we know there's a relationship between the economy and the market, it's difficult to quantify. To better understand this relationship we need to determine what connects one to the other.

Undoubtedly, consumer psychology plays a critical role in determining whether a falling market will significantly affect the real economy. But what role will a falling market have on the psychology of the American consumer today? Though this is a difficult question, we must try to answer it. My concern is that the next bear market will cause consumption to slow to the point where deflation begins. This scenario could wreak havoc on the psychology of the overleveraged American consumer, leading to a dramatic decline in the real economy.

Optimists will surely point to 1987 as an example of the resilience of the American economy. In spite of the stock market crash, consumer confidence held up, Americans continued to spend. No recession developed. So why worry about the market today? On the surface our situation doesn't look that different from 1987. The stock market may be expensive by historical standards but it continues to rise. The American consumer may have lots of debt but continues to spend. Corporate America is prosperous. Unemployment is low. Why is our current situation any more dangerous than it was in 1987?

Americans today have over 30 percent of their net worth in the market (see Figure 5-1). By contrast, during the crash of 1987 stocks accounted for less than 15 percent of household wealth. Clearly, the American consumer is much more likely to feel the financial impact of a stock market crash today than in 1987.

Also the world economy in 1987 was growing strongly, led by a booming Asia. Today the world economy is much more fragile. Asian economies were devastated during the 1997 crisis and have yet to recover fully. Japan, the most important economy in Asia, is still struggling to emerge from its long recession. In 1998 the Russian economy collapsed and the country essentially defaulted on its foreign debt. Almost immediately, capital fled other emerging markets, putting pressure on their currencies, their stock markets, and their economies. Brazil, the largest economy in South America, suffered a currency crisis in late 1998, leading to sharply higher interest rates. The result was a severe recession in Brazil that is still ongoing. Downward pressure is building throughout many of the economies of South America, a region where growth is already quite fragile.

As we enter the new millenium, only America and Western Europe appear reasonably healthy. Much of the globe faces economic stagnation.

In 1987 inflation was on the rise due to strong economic growth around the world. The stock market crash of 1987 certainly caused some uncertainty but it didn't alter consumers' perceptions of inflation. As a result, they continued to borrow and spend and the economy continued to grow.

But debt makes no sense in an enviroment of deflation. Why borrow money to purchase today what will cost less tomorrow? Today, inflation is steady or falling everywhere in the developed world. Japan already has deflation. In the U.S. and Europe inflation rates remain very low. Those emerging markets with relatively strong currencies, such as China, are also suffering from deflationary pressures. Some emerging market countries have seen their currencies collapse, causing hyperinflation in certain imported goods and dollar-based commodities. In those economies, most people have to spend their entire income on food and other necessities. Even those who have discretionary income are reluctant to pay the exorbitant price for imported luxuries. All these factors are driving down the demand for manufactured goods and commodities across the globe.

In 1987 the U.S. dollar was extremely weak, having fallen about 40 percent over the previous two years against other major currencies (see Figures 5-4 and 5-5). The combination of a weak U.S. currency and healthy foreign economies helped our exports to grow strongly after the crash in 1987. From 1987 to 1989 our exports grew over 40 percent while our imports only grew 15 percent. The result (see Figure 5-6) was an improving balance of trade and a strengthening economy.

Figure 5-4 Exchange Rate: U.S. Dollar vs Major Currencies

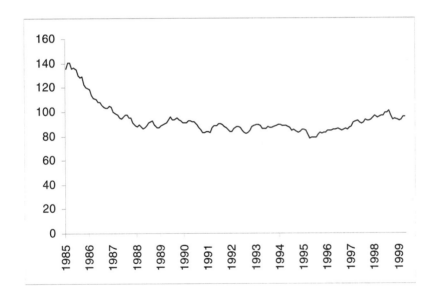

Source: Economagic.com

Figure 5-5 Exchange Rate: U.S. Dollar vs Broad Currency Index

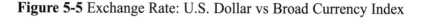

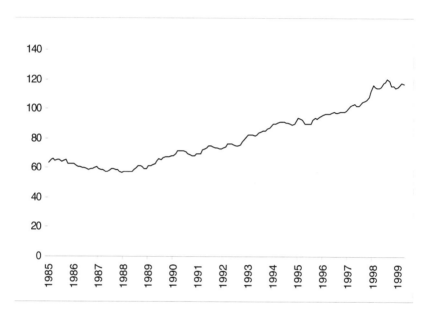

Source: Economagic.com

Today our currency is relatively strong at the same time that many foreign economies are weak. Consequently, though our imports are growing dramatically, our exports stagnate, leading to a record trade deficit.

All these factors suggest that the world economy is much more fragile than it was in 1987. But the crucial difference between today's economy and that of 1987 is clearly the potential for worldwide deflation. Deflation can be devastating for any economy, as we saw in the 1930s and as Japan is experiencing today. However, if deflation hits an economy like ours with a very low savings rate, extremely high consumer debt, and a wildly inflated stock market, the implications for the economy are even more troubling.

Figure 5-6 U.S. Balance Payments: Goods and Services

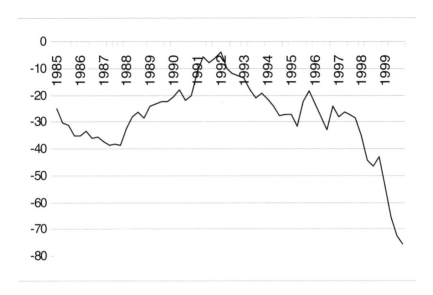

Source: Economagic.com

Perhaps the best way to illustrate this is by comparing our economy to that of Japan. A mere decade ago the Japanese economy was the envy of the world. The Japanese seemed to dominate the production of almost all the important manufactured goods that America wanted to buy. They enjoyed a huge trade surplus in spite of a strong yen. Like most Asian countries, they had a very high personal savings ratio (see Figure 5-7). In virtually every aspect their economy appeared strong, if not invincible, from the standpoint of both the consumer and the corporation. In fact, the Japanese had become so successful that they occupied the role (and still do) of the world's leading creditor nation. This was the same role held by the U.S. in the 1920s.

Figure 5-7 Japanese Personal Savings

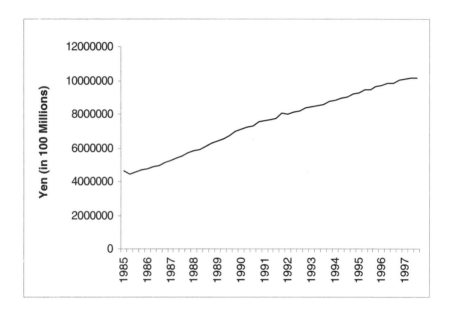

Source: Economagic.com

Unfortunately, these undeniable strengths did not insulate the Japanese from the risks inherent in an asset bubble. The tremendous wealth created in Japan spilled over into stocks and real estate. Eventually these assets became dangerously overpriced and they collapsed as the economy began to lose its strong upward momentum. This is precisely what took place in America in the 1920s and 1930s.

Like the United States in the 1930s, Japan is having a great deal of difficulty escaping the grip of a deflationary economy. Now, a full decade after the Japanese bubble burst, lasting economic recovery remains elusive.

At the heart of this problem lies the Japanese consumer. Japanese consumers have savings of approximately $10 trillion, an average of

roughly $80,000 per person. Yet in spite of this enormous cash cush-
ion the Japanese economy continues to stagnate. Why?

First, Japanese consumers are very different from their American
counterparts. The Japanese have always been big savers. The prolonged weakness in the Japanese stock market and real estate market
has only reinforced the Japanese consumer's cautious outlook (see
Figure 5-8). More importantly, the deflationary environment there
encourages savings at the expense of consumption. So in spite of the
enormous capacity for Japanese consumers to stimulate the economy,
people save and the economy stagnates.

Figure 5-8 Japanese Consumer Confidence

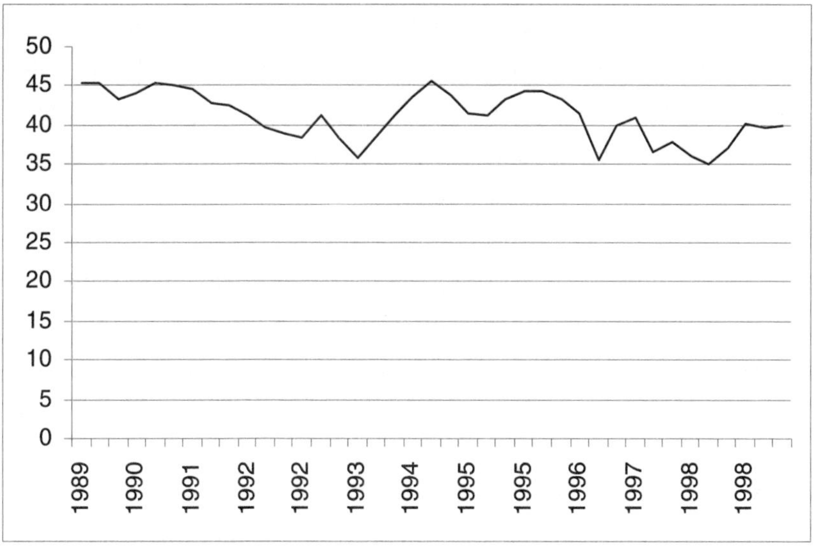

Source: Economagic.com

Second, Japanese corporations played a major role in the boom
that occurred in the 1980s. The incredible success of the Japanese

export machine led corporations to build enormous amounts of new production capacity, anticipating continued strong growth in the demand for their products. A great deal of this production capacity was financed with debt. In fact, a similar phenomenon appeared throughout Asia in the 1980s and early 1990s.

Today, growth in demand no longer exists. The combination of a faltering world economy and brutal price competition means that much of Japanese production capacity is simply unprofitable. There is certainly no need to build new capacity. The result is that both the consumer sector and the corporate sector in Japan are contracting. In this situation the Japanese only have one card left to play: government spending. They are playing this card at the moment. We can only hope that it works.

As bad as this situation is, imagine how much worse it would be if Japanese consumers had lots of debt rather than lots of savings. The large surplus of savings at least gives them the wherewithal to solve their problem—if consumers would only import some of America's excess optimism. Unfortunately, as we have already seen, consumer psychology is highly unpredictable.

Now consider our own situation. Consumer spending accounts for roughly two thirds of the American economy today. The consumer thus has a critical role in the future of the U.S. economy. But unlike their Japanese counterparts, American consumers can't fall back on savings if the economy contracts. Americans have only about $6 trillion in savings (see Figure 5-9). This amounts to an average of about $25,000 per person. At the same time Americans have $1.4 trillion of consumer credit outstanding (see Figure 5-10) *in addition to* mortgage debt and auto lease payments. All together total household debt exceeded $6 trillion in 1999.[1]

---

[1] *Wall Street Journal*, July 5, 2000 "Debtor Nation" pg c1.

Figure 5-9 U.S. Household Savings

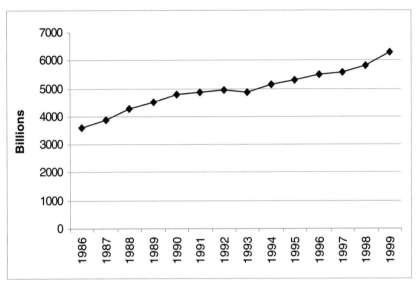

Source: Federal Reserve Board Flow of Funds

Figure 5-10 Consumer Credit Outstanding

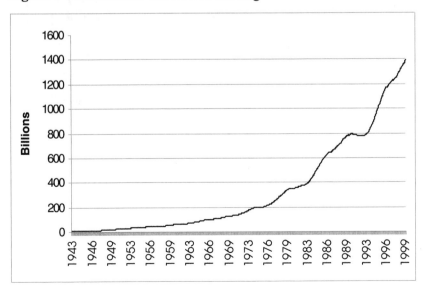

Source: Economagic.com

In a deflationary economy the American consumer will strive to pay off debt costing 8 to 20 percent per annum, using savings that are only earning 2 to 5 percent per annum. This will be a difficult task for most Americans. The wallet of the average consumer today is already stretched about as far as it can go. Debt service payments as a percent of income are close to the all-time high reached during the recession of 1990 (see Figure 5-11), and in spite of a growing economy bankruptcy filings have soared in recent years (see Figure 5-12).

Figure 5-11 Debt Service vs Disposable Personal Income

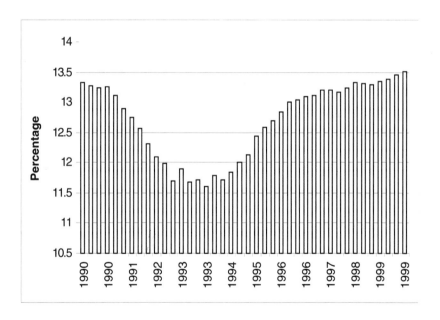

Source: Economagic.com

Figure 5-12 Personal Bankruptcies

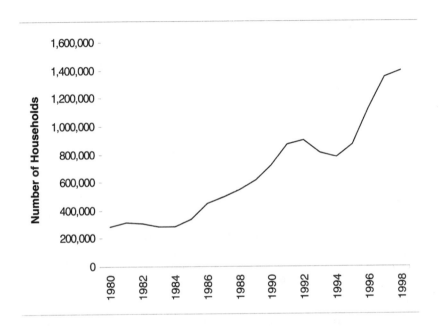

Source: American Bankruptcy Institute

Most Americans will find there are only two ways to reduce debt: liquidate long- term investments (stocks) or cut spending. In either case, the result will be downward pressure on the stock market and the economy. The consequence may well be a vicious downward spiral in consumer spending, leading to a severe contraction in the economy.

Bullish analysts insist that America has entered a new era of non-inflationary growth driven by the increasing productivity of our technology-based economy. Clearly, technology has played a crucial role in raising productivity and lowering inflation. But these factors do not account for the tremendous strength of consumer spending in America. Indeed, debt accumulation has been the main driver of our consumer-based economy in the 1990s.

Historically speaking, this is not at all unusual. Most economic booms are fueled by rapid debt accumulation. The Asian Miracle of the 1980s was certainly due in part to the explosion of corporate debt in that part of the world. Japan, Korea, and several other Asian nations are currently struggling to recover from the excessive debt burdens accumulated by corporations in the 1980s and 1990s.

The statistics on consumer debt, personal bankruptcies, and household liquidity ratios all point to a consumer who is over-leveraged and extremely vulnerable (see Figure 5-13). The strains on the economy caused by excessive debt growth are already apparent. Personal bankruptcies and corporate bond defaults are reaching levels usually reserved for recessions. Yet this is the longest post-war expansion on record, a time when we would expect both personal and corporate balance sheets to be rock solid. Clearly, the U.S. economy is not as healthy as it appears to be. Excessive debt is slowly eroding our economic foundation.

At the moment the world economy is largely being held together by the optimism of the American consumer. The buoyancy provided by this demand is like a firewall, protecting our economy from the flames encroaching on our borders. But can we depend on the American consumer to maintain that buoyant attitude? Sooner or later the optimism will erode. If this should happen before Japan can resume its growth, the risk of global deflation will increase dramatically.

Figure 5-13 Influence of Total Consumer Debt on Bankruptcy
Filing Trends by Year 1980-1997

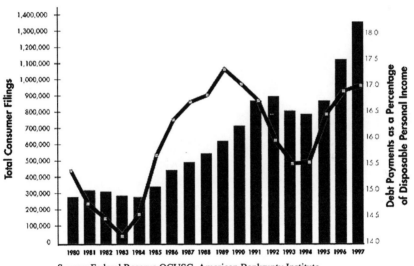

Source: Federal Reserve OCUSC, American Bankrupty Institute

6

DISTURBING SIGNS

The asset bubble in the U.S. stock market did not appear overnight. Indeed, this problem has been building since 1996. However, the deflation risk has escalated much more rapidly. That risk has grown exponentially over the last couple of years due to several events: the Asian economic crisis of late 1997, the Russian debt default of 1998, and most recently the Brazilian currency crisis of late 1998.

The Asian crisis began in Thailand and quickly spread across the region, encompassing Malaysia, Indonesia, Korea, and a host of other nations. Initially, the crisis was dismissed by many analysts as an isolated event that would have little impact on the U.S. These analysts assumed that because Asia represented a relatively small percentage of U.S. exports, the impact here would be contained and short-lived.

This view of the crisis failed to recognize that Asia represents almost a third of the world's economy. To believe that the entire region could fall into recession or depression almost overnight without a profound impact on the world economy requires excessive optimism and a lack of common sense. The nations of the world today are connected by trade flows (goods) and capital flows (money) as never before. The severity of the Asian crisis almost guaranteed a disruption in these trade and capital flows and posed an extraordinary risk to the world economy.

Beyond all this, the Asian crisis is extremely important in that it complicates Japan's task of escaping from its economic slump. Japanese corporations have lots of investments throughout Asia. These investments will now provide no economic return for some time. Japanese banks also have been big lenders in the region. They can ill afford to absorb their losses elsewhere in Asia given all the troubles they have at home. The result is that Japan is likely to pull back from its enormous investments (both equity and debt) in the region and concentrate on the domestic economy. This will prolong the adjustment period necessary to solve the region's problems.

Indeed, there's already evidence that Japanese banks and corporations are beginning to pull back across the globe. Bank of Tokyo Mitsubishi, the largest and strongest Japanese bank, sold part of its interest in the Union Bank of California. Nissan, Japan's second largest automobile manufacturer, recently concluded negotiations to sell off a large equity stake to foreign investors.

It's like a game of global Monopoly: Japanese banks and some Japanese corporations need cash. To raise that cash they're selling or mortgaging their overseas properties. As the world's leading creditor nation, Japan plays a crucial role in financing growth around the globe, but currently Japan is pulling back from that role as it tries to solve its domestic problems. To maintain growth, the world needs a new lender to take the place of the Japanese. Unfortunately, no other country seems capable of fulfilling that role.

The Russian debt default almost overnight shifted the crisis from a regional to a potentially global one. From a purely economic standpoint the Russian collapse may appear less significant than the Asian. After all, the Russian economy is far smaller than the combined economies of Asia. However, the global impact of the Russian problem goes far beyond the purely economic considerations. The very real potential for economic and political chaos in a military superpower like Russia evokes fears about the stability of all Europe. Moreover, Western European banks have been the biggest lenders to Russia; they must absorb the losses suffered there. Overall, Europe appears fairly healthy at the moment. However, the new Euro currency has got off to a weak start since it was introduced in 1999. Monetary union is a grand experiment fraught with risk. It will be some time before we know if it will succeed.

Equally important is the negative impact that the Russian situation has had in other emerging market economies. Foreign investors sharply reduced their exposure in all emerging markets after being stung with large losses in Russia. This large outflow of capital caused severe currency weakness (as is often the case) in many of these countries; the most important of which is Brazil.

The Brazilian currency collapse threatened to engulf all of South America in an economic crisis like the Asian one. The leading economic powers and the International Monetary Fund (IMF) recognized that the global risks were getting out of control. Mobilizing, they fairly quickly put together a large economic aid package that for a time calmed the frayed nerves of the markets—and investors.

But Brazil's problems were already beyond anyone's control. After a few short months, investor confidence faded again and capital began leaving the country. Brazil simply didn't have the reserves to defend its currency. The country was forced to devalue. Brazil suffered a sharp recession and now faces a difficult recovery. In fact, many other South American countries have experienced economic and political crisis since the Brazilian collapse. Amazingly, many analysts reacted to the Brazilian crisis with the same shallow arguments heard after the Asian and Russian crises. What these analysts fail to see is that all of these events are connected by the growing deflationary risks we face.

So where does this leave us? In mid-1997, the world economy, growing almost everywhere, appeared stable. Today more than a third of the world is in recession or stagnation and almost every economy appears fragile. Even the U.S., which on the surface appears relatively strong, is beginning to show significant signs of stress. The most obvious signs are a sharp slowdown in corporate profit growth and greatly increased volatility in the financial markets. Unfortunately, deflationary signals are becoming increasingly apparent in our economy.

Figure 6-1 Producer Price Index: All Commodities

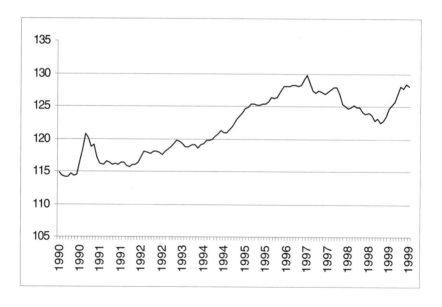

Source: Economagic.com

Some of these deflationary pressures are quite obvious, like the dramatic drop in commodity prices. Since the Asian crisis hit, broad commodity indexes have dropped sharply and still show few signs of recovery (see Figure 6-1).

Oil prices rebounded significantly in 1999, but that's due primarily to reduced OPEC supply rather than any real improvement in demand (see Figure 6-2). While commodities play a smaller role in today's economy than they once did, they continue to be an excellent barometer of global economic health. The persistent weakness in commodity prices is a clear signal that global demand is soft.

Figure 6-2 Oil Price

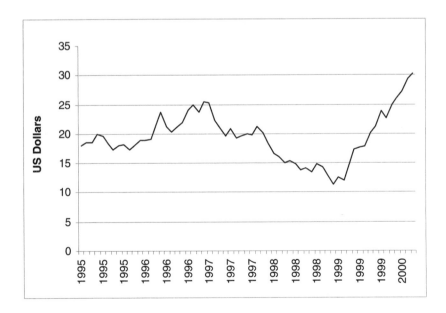

Source: Economagic.com

One of the most surprising and least discussed signs of deflation has been the tremendous weakness in the prices of real estate investment trusts (REITs) (see Figure 6-3). Normally these stocks trade like utilities, moving up as interest rates fall and falling as rates rise, primarily due to the typical REITs need to borrow money for growth. In 1998, the opposite occurred: Though interest rates fell dramatically, REIT prices dropped more than 20 percent. This is very unusual because the high dividends (5 to 10 percent) that REITs pay out should be coveted when interest rates are falling. The obvious implication of declining REIT prices is that the market expects real estate values to begin falling, perhaps brought down by reduced occupancy rates and lower cash flows. In other words, the market expects deflation to spread beyond commodities to other hard assets.

Figure 6-3 REIT (Real Estate Investment Trust) Index

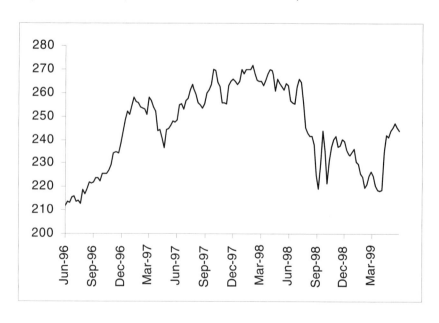

Source: Microsoft Investor / CSI Inc.

Some may argue that the weakness in REITs is due to other factors, such as the growing importance of the Internet. Some analysts expect the surging popularity of e-commerce to reduce the need for retail outlets. Since many REITs do indeed own substantial amounts of retail space in the form of shopping malls, this explanation does make some sense.

However, after looking at many different types of REITs I began to realize that the Internet alone couldn't account for the declining prices of publicly traded REITs. All types of REITs were falling, regardless of whether they had any shopping malls. Even REITs that specialize in golf courses were falling fairly rapidly. Clearly, the broad weakness in REITs can't be blamed on the Internet.

Some analysts "explained" that the growing credit crunch was reducing the availability of credit to the REIT industry. Once again this argument has some logic. There were clear signs of widening credit spreads after the collapse of Long-Term Capital, the hedge fund. If REITs had difficulty borrowing money, then financing their growth would become more costly. However, even the financially strong REITs, those with little need to access capital markets, were weakening.

While the credit crunch and the Internet may account for some of the weakness in REIT prices, neither is sufficient to justify the extreme, broad-based decline in REITs during 1998 and 1999 (see Figure 6-3). In my estimation, growing deflationary expectations are the primary cause of the REIT collapse.

The most ominous deflationary signal is one that has received a lot of attention from Fed Chairman Greenspan. "Credit crunch" is a term that many Americans may not be very familiar with. It refers to a situation where credit becomes less available or more costly to borrowers. Periodically, banks and other lenders become cautious due to a weak economy, more defaults among borrowers, or both. The typical response is for lenders to raise rates for less creditworthy borrowers and shut off credit entirely to the weakest ones. This situation, a credit crunch, often arises during a recession. What's so unusual about the credit crunch of late 1998 is that it occurred during a period of general economic expansion. Chairman Greenspan himself stated that he had never witnessed a period of risk aversion like this in his lifetime.

The most obvious sign of the recent credit crunch is the large spread between rates on government debt and rates on lower-quality (junk) debt. These yield spreads, as they're called, typically widen during recessions, because investors become concerned about the ability of less creditworthy borrowers to fulfill their obligations. During these periods, investors flock to the highest-quality government bonds. This process causes government bonds to rise (yields fall) and junk bond prices to fall (yields rise), thereby increasing "spreads." As you can see from Figure 6-4, yield spreads widened dramatically after the Asian crisis in late 1997. The last time they were this wide was during the savings and loan crisis and recession of 1990.

The recent credit crunch illustrates that the U.S. banking system no longer has exclusive control over the availability of credit in our economy, even though for the last several years the banking system has been generous (by any standard) in providing credit. The crisis shows that other lenders can behave differently than the banks, thereby undermining the influence of the central bank.

Who are these other lenders? Basically most Americans are lenders, whether they know it or not. Any investor who buys a bond or a package of bonds (bond fund or unit investment trust) becomes a lender.

The last time you bought a car or a house, it's likely that you got a loan from a bank. However, there's a good chance that the originating bank sold your loan, as well as many others, to a group of investors. Should you default on your loan, the loser in the transaction is this group of investors rather than the originating bank.

Figure 6-4 Yield Spread: Government vs Single B Corp.

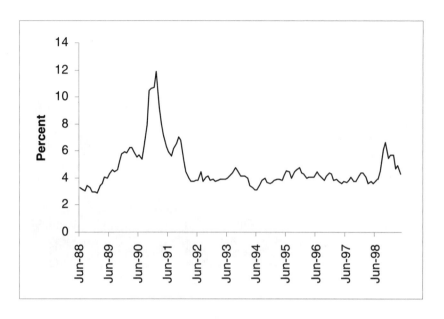

Source: Global Financial Data

The process through which banks package loans together and sell them to investors is known as *securitization*. Securitization has grown dramatically since the bull market began in 1982, fueled both by the desire of banks to disperse certain credit risks to other lenders and the growing appetite of investors for the higher yields available on diversified portfolios of corporate or personal debt (see Figure 6-5).

Corporations are also less dependent on banks today than they were in earlier decades. Today, when a corporation needs money, it's far more likely to turn to Wall Street to underwrite a bond or stock offering than to go to a bank.

Figure 6-5 Securitized Assets

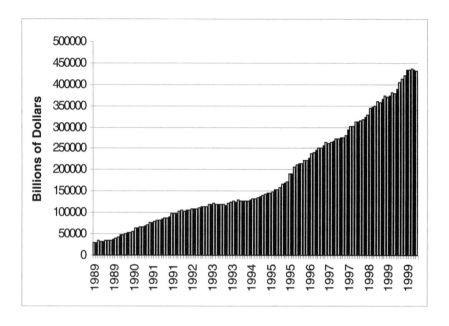

Source: Economagic.com

The significance of this is that we live in an economy that is far less dependent on banks and far more dependent on investor psychology than at any time in our history. The recent credit crunch seems to have emanated from weakness in investor psychology, not from any stinginess on the part of traditional lenders. This is a dramatic departure from the credit cycles we were accustomed to in the past. It also represents a new risk to the U.S. economy. The unavoidable conclusion here is that when the economy does eventually begin to weaken, the Fed, working through commercial banks, will be less able to stimulate demand than it has been in the past.

Most investors today assume that the Fed has the power to control the economy by raising or lowering rates. Indeed, after the fallout from the Long-Term Capital collapse and the Russian crisis, the Federal Reserve, working with central banks around the world, initiated a series of global interest rate cuts. This unprecedented easing of monetary policy quickly led the Dow to rebound from 7,500 to over 9,000 and caused credit spreads to decline. Clearly, most investors still have faith that the Fed will work its magic on the global economy.

This optimism may no longer be justified. In Japan, where banks are still dominant in providing credit, the central bank has essentially failed in its attempt to stimulate the economy by lowering rates. With long-term rates there now below 2 percent, monetary policy is no longer an effective tool. The central bank's efforts have been overwhelmed by the lack of consumer confidence and the consequences of a deflationary environment. It should be clear that we would be even more vulnerable if consumer confidence should erode here in the U.S.

With the Dow now above 10,000 and most markets around the world rising, it appears that the Central Bank cuts were very effective in restoring confidence to the financial markets. But will they result in real economic recovery in Asia and other parts of the world? The jury is still out.

No book dealing with today's bull market would be complete without a discussion of the Internet. The Internet is relevant to this book in two critical aspects.

First, the incredible speculation in Internet stocks is a clear sign that our market has become completely detached from economic reality. In fact the Internet stock craze may well go down as the most speculative period in the history of U.S. financial markets. It's quite possible that our children and grandchildren will remember today's Internet craze in the same way we remember the Dutch Tulip mania: as the most extreme and absurd speculation imaginable.

The other, perhaps more significant, reason that the Internet is important is that it could become one of the most powerful deflationary forces that we have ever encountered.

The term "mania" is defined in Webster's Dictionary as "madness." I can think of no better word to describe the mentality of today's typical Internet investor. While most investors understand that Internet stocks are expensive and inherently volatile, few appreciate the magnitude of the speculation in these stocks. I could cite a slew of Internet initial public offerings (IPOs) that doubled, tripled, or even quintupled in their first day of trading. Literally overnight these tiny companies became worth more than most companies that were 10 or even 20 times their size. Netscape was the first such company to grab investors' attention as an IPO, but many others have followed.

The shares of several companies have skyrocketed in price just on the announcement that they would, in some way, become involved in the Internet. One of the more interesting of these was Zapata, a company that generates most of its revenues from fishmeal. On announcing that it was going into the Internet business, its shares promptly rose from 9 to 25 in two days (see Figure 7-1). Fishmeal to the Internet, sounds logical, doesn't it?

Figure 7-1 Zapata Corp. (ZAP)

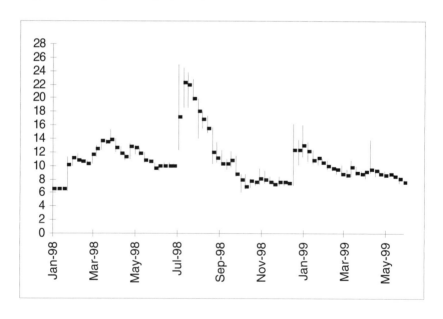

Source Microsoft Investor / CSI Inc.

Perhaps the most amazing of all, at least so far, is a company called Avtel Communications. This stock skyrocketed from 2 to 30 in a single day, a rise of over 1,200 percent, on the announcement that it would offer high speed Internet access in California. Perhaps this rise would be justified if the service was unique. It is not.

Two recent offerings provide a glimpse of the giddy environment for Internet-related IPOs. Sycamore Networks (see Figure 7-2) gets the prize for sporting the highest market capitalization after its first day of trading: $14.4 billion. A few days later the stock had reached $251 a share; the offering price had been $38. At that point the stock had a market capitalization of over $18 billion—on sales of $11.3 million. The price/sales ratio was 1,600!

Figure 7-2 Sycamore Chart Adjusted for Splits

The following week Akamai Technologies (see Figure 7-3) went public at $26 a share and ended the day at over $145. At that price the market capitalization of the company was about $13 billion—on revenue of $1.3 million for the first nine months of 1999. On its first day of trading, this tiny company had a stock-market valuation larger than Sears, Roebuck & Co.!

Figure 7-3 Akamai Technologies Chart

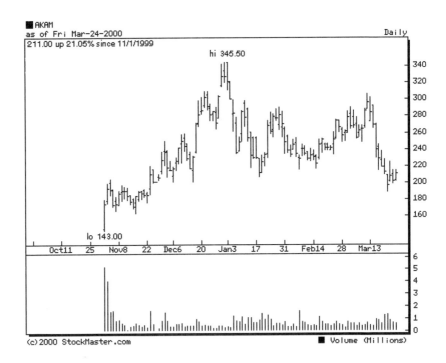

While all these stories make for interesting reading, by themselves they tell us little about the risk of the overall market. In the past there has been extreme speculation in many individual stocks. In most cases these same stocks (like the biotech stocks of the mid-1980s) suffered impressive collapses when reality fell well short of investors' high expectations. However, these speculative episodes usually had little impact on the direction of the market as a whole; they remained isolated pockets of speculation in an otherwise rational environment.

By contrast, this bull market seems to be dominated by speculation, with isolated pockets of rationality. Since 1995 speculation has increased markedly, moving from the tech stocks to the large capitalization growth stocks, and now back again to the technology arena.

Undoubtedly, the Internet represents the zenith of speculation within the technology group. Collectively, Internet stocks represent a tidal wave of speculation that has been building for many years. When this wave eventually crashes, it's likely to leave broad devastation in its wake.

One way to comprehend this speculation is to look at the dollars involved. While it would be impractical to identify all of the publicly traded Internet stocks, I have singled out four of them to illustrate a point. I chose Amazon (Figure 7-4), America Online (Figure 7-5), E-Bay (Figure 7-6), and Yahoo (Figure 7-7) because they're among the most established Internet stocks today.

Collectively, AOL, Amazon, E-Bay, and Amazon have been publicly traded for a total of only 10 years. At the end of 1998 they had combined revenues totaling just over $4 billion and earnings of $108 million. Yet today these stocks have a combined market value of over $191 billion. They're now trading at 46 times revenue and over 1,700 times last year's earnings. Clearly, Wall Street is optimistic about the future earnings prospects for these companies. In fact earnings are expected to grow to $547 million in 2000. These optimistic earnings forecasts leave us with a P/E ratio of 349 for 2000.

Figure 7-4 Amazon Chart

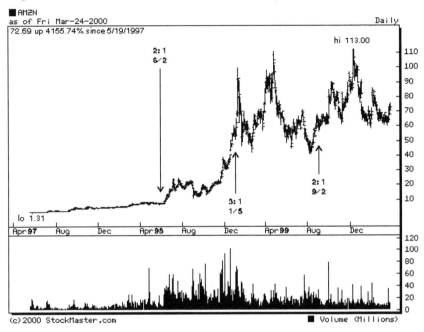

Figure 7-5 America Online Chart

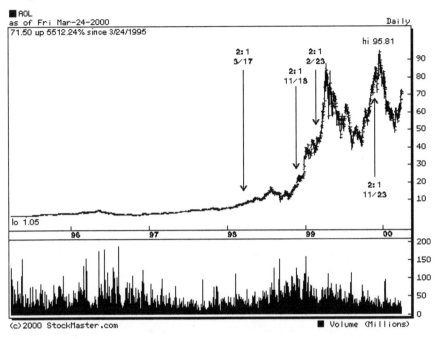

■ AOL
as of Fri Mar-24-2000   Daily
71.50 up 5512.24% since 3/24/1995

(c) 2000 StockMaster.com   ■ Volume (Millions)

	Earnings Per Share Next Expected EPS Date: Apr 18						
	93–4	94–5	95–6	96–7	97–8	98–9	99–0
Sep	.00	.00	.00	.02	.01	.03	.07
Dec	.00	.00	.01	−.04	.01	.04	.09
Mar	.00	.00	.01	.01	.02	.05	
Jun	.00	.00	.01	.01	.03	.07	
	.01	.01	.03	−.01	.07	.18	
Yr. to Yr.	129 %	123 %	−132 %	800 %	150 %		

(Quarterly numbers may not add to annuals)

Figure 7-6 E-Bay Chart

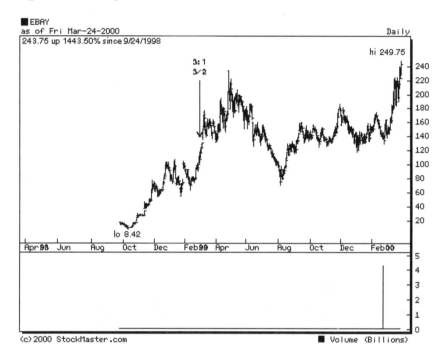

	1993	1994	1995	1996	1997	1998	1999
Earnings Per Share							
Next Expected EPS Date: Apr 24							
Mar	—	—	—	—	.00	.01	.05
Jun	—	—	—	—	.01	.02	.04
Sep	—	—	—	—	.00	.02	.02
Dec	—	—	—	—	.00	.02	.04
					.02	.07	.15
Yr. to Yr.					—	367 %	114 %

(Quarterly numbers may not add to annuals)

Figure 7-7 Yahoo Chart

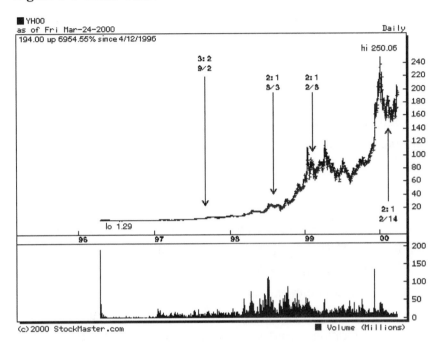

(c) 2000 StockMaster.com   ■ Volume (Millions)

	1993	1994	1995	1996	1997	1998	1999
Mar	—	—	—	.00	.00	−.01	.03
Jun	—	—	—	−.01	.00	−.01	.05
Sep	—	—	—	−.01	.00	.01	.07
Dec	—	—	—	.00	.01	.02	.10
				−.01	.01	.02	.25
Yr. to Yr.				—	138 %	200 %	.25

Earnings Per Share
Next Expected EPS Date: Apr 05

(Quarterly numbers may not add to annuals)

Is this rational? Consider what it means. Let's assume these companies do earn $547 million in 2000, and they continue to earn $547 million every year thereafter. Let's also assume they pay out all their earnings as dividends. At today's prices, that means an investor will receive all his money back in 349 years. In other words, an investor stands to break even in 2348. Talk about investing for the long term!

Bulls will argue that these companies will continue to grow earnings rapidly for many years, making the payback period much shorter than 349 years. Perhaps so, but the competition is extraordinary in this rapidly changing industry. An awful lot can happen in 349 years. Can we have confidence in earnings expectations five or 10 years out, let alone 349 years? Can we even be confident that these companies will still be around? The fact that investors are willing to look that far into the future for a return on their investment is testimony to the giddiness of the current environment.

These valuations are so extreme that it's difficult to put them into any kind of rational context. How can earnings for these top-tier Internet stocks possibly grow fast enough to justify current prices? That's why analysts tend to ignore all traditional valuation methods and look for other, more subjective, reasons to buy these stocks. One such valuation tool measures the number of "hits," or page views, recorded by each company's Web site. And when will these hits translate into revenues, or even earnings?

Indeed, one of the hallmarks of this bull market is the willingness of certain analysts, and many investors, to look beyond traditional valuation measures and adopt new rules. These rules are much less restrictive than the old ones. They have to be, if they're to justify prices that are rising, in some cases at exponential rates. While the new rules may occasionally be apparent in other sectors of the market, they're simply taken for granted in discussing Internet valuations.

These new valuation methods are difficult to criticize precisely because they're so subjective. Ultimately, though, investors who throw out all objective forms of analysis will find themselves lost without a compass. When this tidal wave of speculation finally breaks, these investors won't have the faintest idea whether they're looking at another great buying opportunity or their last chance to desert a sinking ship. Many may reason that a stock that has dropped from 100 to 50 must be a decent value, when any rational analysis would value the stock no higher than 5.

If we can't find any rational justification for current prices by looking at earnings or tangible assets, perhaps we should look at the other assets of Internet companies. Certainly, one of the most important assets of the Internet companies is their employees. In Table 7-1 I've tried to compare the Internet stocks to some other extremely successful companies by looking at the value we place on their employees. A simple ratio (market capitalization / number of employees) tells us how much investors are paying for each employee.

Table 7-1: Highly Valued Employees

Internet Stocks:	Market Capitalization / # of Employees
Amazon	$10 million
AOL	$13 million
Yahoo	$42 million
EBAY	$244 million
Internet composite (all four)	$16 million
Other Companies:	
INTEL	$3 million
Coca Cola	$5 million
Microsoft	$16 million
(Valuation as of 3/26/99)	

Source: Microsoft Investor

As you can see, investors today are placing valuations on these Internet companies that imply their employees are each worth $16 million. This makes them far more expensive that the employees of Intel or Coca Cola, who are by no means cheap. In effect, investors are saying that they expect all of these Internet companies to be as successful and as profitable as Microsoft. The odds of this are quite remote.

There are plenty of other Internet stocks that trade at equally expensive valuations. Anthony and Michael Perkins in *The Internet Bubble*[1] tell us that in the spring of 1999 a portfolio of 133 Internet stocks had a market capitalization of $410 billion, sales of $15.2 billion, and losses of $3.2 billion. That translates into a price/sales ratio of approximately 27, an extraordinary statistic. As you can see from Figure 7-8, $410 billion exceeds the value of many of the stock markets around the world.

True, the Internet is a growth industry and some of these companies will become highly profitable. But it's also true that many of these companies will eventually fail. Competition will insure that. For while the Internet holds great promise, it is and will continue to be highly competitive. None of these companies have patents, as do the pharmaceutical companies, to protect them from competition. New competitors don't need much capital to enter the market, as they do in the automobile of the semiconductor industry. In short, the barriers to entry in the Internet industry are low and the pace of change is extraordinarily high. It all adds up to a highly unpredictable group of stocks to invest in.

---

[1] Harper Business, 1999,

Figure 7-8 Martket Capitalization of Selected World Markets: 12/98

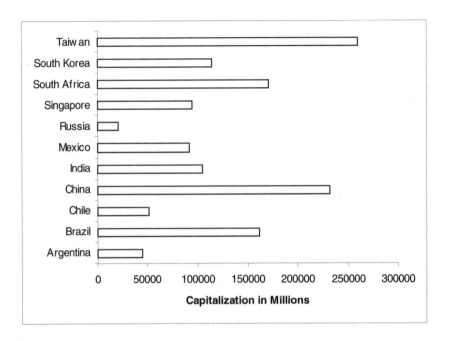

Source: Global Financial Data

Recently I saw an interview on CNBC dealing with e-commerce stocks. These are companies like Amazon that sell all kinds of things over the Internet. The interviewer logically questioned the value of Amazon, which has skyrocketed in price while generating huge operating losses. The guest analyst argued that at this point in its development the company *should* be investing heavily in its future and should not be expected to earn money. He went on to say that he would sell the stock if they started to make money. He actually wanted them to lose money! This kind of thinking typifies the irrationality in today's market.

A company that can't turn a profit with exceptional sales growth is going to have an even more difficult time when competition heats up and sales growth slows. Furthermore, companies like Amazon are going to have an extremely difficult time differentiating their products and generating customer loyalty. If you walk into Borders or Barnes & Noble to buy a book, the store conveys a certain atmosphere that may well keep you coming back. But someone who goes to the Internet to purchase is likely to be concerned about only two things: expediency and price. Amazon has achieved tremendous sales growth because it had a head start on the competition. As their competitors improve, Amazon's sales growth will slow and price competition will intensify. Profitability will remain elusive.

As the Internet becomes easier and faster to use, the issue of price competition will come to the fore. Consumers will find that they can quickly compare prices from several retailers at the touch of a key. This may well alter retailing in a profound way. Consumers will ultimately gain influence and control at the expense of retailers. As profit margins erode, deflationary pressures will rise. While these trends may be good for consumers, they could be disastrous for investors.

I have no doubt that online retailing will grow dramatically in the years ahead. However as it does, it's likely to facilitate increased price competition in many industries. What's good for consumers may be very bad for corporations looking to turn a profit. Many investors today don't see that risk—that online retailing will intensify the deflationary forces already at work in our economy. Internet stocks, an investor's dream today, may soon become the investor's worst nightmare.

Who will be hurt when Internet stocks collapse? Surprisingly mutual funds and other institutional investors don't control these stocks (see Figure 7-9). So far, it's largely the individual investor who is buying these securities.

Figure 7-9 Institutional Share of Total NYSE Volume

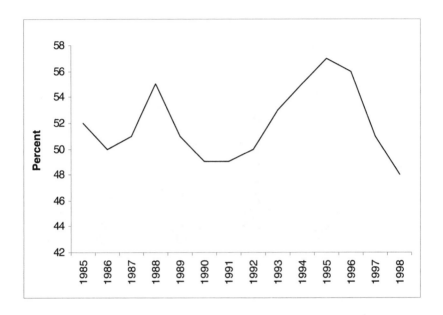

Source: The Wall Street Journal 11/16/98, "Abreast of the Market,: pg. c1

The role of the individual investor in the market has been growing for several years now, especially in the technology arena (see Figure 7-10). This trend has been fueled by the explosive growth of online trading and the emergence of fee-based investment accounts, which can dramatically reduce transaction costs. Online trading gives individuals two tools necessary to trade stocks that until now were only possessed by institutions: (1) quick access to information, and (2) low commissions.

Figure 7-10 Small Trades (less than 1,000 shares)

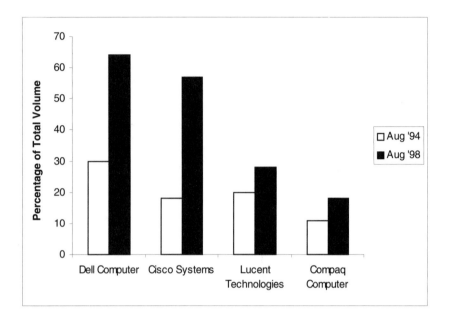

Source: The Wall Street Journal 11/16/98, "Abreast of the Market,: pg. c1

Individuals have flocked to the technology stocks for obvious reasons. First, technology stocks have led the bull market of the 1990s. Beginning with the hype associated with the introduction of Windows 95, the technology group produced many stocks that appeared to have unlimited growth potential. From 1992 to 1995 most of these were in the semiconductor and software fields. Stocks like Micron Technology and LSI Logic simply exploded during this period (see Figure 7-11). But as semiconductor stocks peaked in 1995, leadership began to move to Internet stocks. By 1997, companies like America Online, Amazon, Yahoo and other Internet stocks had become America's hottest stocks (see Figures 7-4 to 7-7).

Figure 7-11a LSI Logic (LSI)

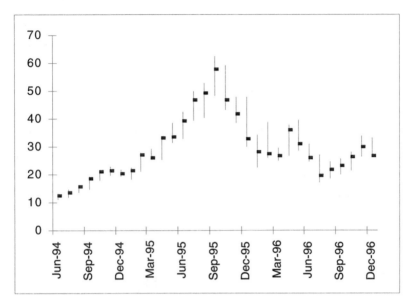

Figure 7-11b Micron Technology (MU)

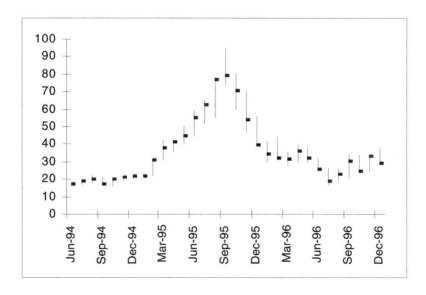

Source: Microsoft Investor / CSI Inc.

There's no denying that the technology sector has been the main source of growth for the U.S. economy during the nineties. Many leading technology companies have experienced phenomenal growth rates, justifying above-average P/E ratios and market capitalizations. It's therefore quite rational that growth-oriented investors have gravitated toward technology stocks.

But are the people buying these stocks long-term investors who truly understand the risks? Or are they, by and large, short-term speculators looking for a quick profit? The answer is unambiguous. According to a recent study by Bain & Co., shareholders of Amazon typically hold their stock for 10 and shareholders of Yahoo 11 days (see Figure 7-12).

Figure 7-12 Average Holding Period (NYSE)

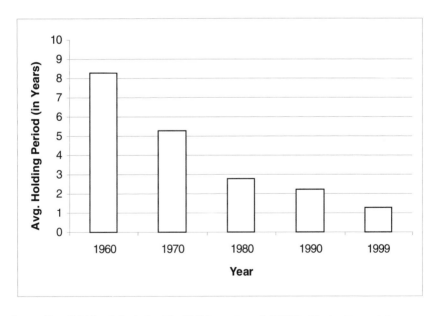

Source: Darrell Rigby, Bain & Co., The Wall Street Journal, 11/2/99, "Getting Personal: Investor Relationships Fade Fast"

My worst fears about the Internet mania were confirmed during a recent visit to a Chinese restaurant. While waiting for my take-out order I struck up a conversation with the bartender, who asked where I worked. On learning that I was a financial advisor, the bartender divulged that she was day-trading stocks through a discount broker. My curiosity was piqued. I had heard a lot of stories about day-traders but I had never actually met one. I asked which stocks she traded. She responded "America Online, Amazon, Yahoo, and Lucent." In other words three Internet stocks and one Internet-related stock. Alas, my food was ready and our conversation ended. But on the way home I couldn't help but wonder how many other day-traders across the country are buying and selling the same stocks.

Alan Greenspan summed up this mania quite well when he recently compared buying Internet stocks to buying lottery tickets: "Investors are ignoring the overwhelming probability that they will lose money and instead focusing on the very small possibility of hitting the jackpot."

While the pure Internet sector clearly represents the most extreme example of speculation in our market today, it's by no means the only sector. Speculation is rampant throughout the universe of technology stocks, especially those that are expected to benefit as Internet usage grows. Valuations for these stocks, most of which trade on the NASDAQ market, have reached absurd levels. We've witnessed similar bouts of speculation throughout America's history when exciting new industries emerged: biotechs in the 1980s, automobile stocks in the early 1900s, railroads in the late 1800s. All these speculative episodes ended very badly for investors.

But today's Internet mania is not just about investors losing sight of valuations. It's about investors turning into speculators. Across America, "value" investing is giving way to "momentum" investing. This is the investment strategy used by most day-traders: Instead of analyzing the value of a stock, investors simply identify stocks with the greatest upward momentum and buy them. These same stocks are sold when the upward momentum begins to fade or reverse. The actual holding period could be as short as an hour or two (see Figure 7-13). The value or worth of a company is not a consideration to momentum investors.

Figure 7-13 Dollar Trading vs GDP

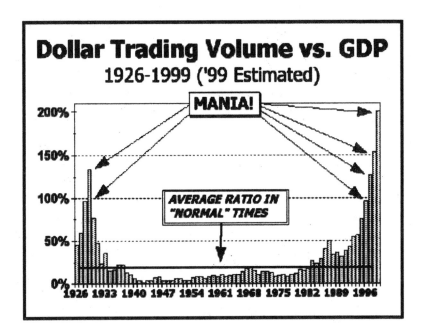

Source: Courtesy of HD BROUS & Co., Inc.

This style of "investing" is common during periods of extreme speculation. It was prevalent in Japan in the late 1980s and in America in the late 1920s. Evidence of the trend today is readily apparent. The magnitude of the changes that have occurred is clear (see Figures 7-12 and 7-13). Investors are holding stocks for shorter and shorter periods, even on the more conservative NYSE. The result has been an explosion of trading volume relative to gross domestic product (GDP), far surpassing the mania of the late 1920s.

This unfortunate trend will backfire. Eventually these speculators will realize that they've been gambling, not investing. The stock market will be recognized as a casino rather than an efficient mechanism for the creation of long-term capital.

CHAPTER

8

DEFLATION AND YOUR INVESTMENTS

Over the years I've found that investment advice from books is often of limited value, partly because by the time the book makes it to press, the financial markets may have changed considerably. More important, we're all very different when it comes to our investment inclinations. Some of us are very aggressive, others are conservative; some of us have a short-term orientation, others long-term. And unfortunately some of us are really not sure what we are. So what may be good advice for one person turns out to be not so good advice for another. For these reasons individual investors might be better off ignoring most of the advice in books, especially when it concerns individual stocks or market sectors.

Having said this, it still seems ludicrous to write a book about the perils of deflation without mentioning its implications for investment portfolios. The fact that there has been no deflation for 60 years means that, if it appears, it's likely to take most people by surprise. Living with inflation, people have developed investing habits, as well as lifestyle habits, over a very long period of time. At times inflation has been rampant, as it was in the 1970s. Usually it's been much more tame. Nonetheless we have learned to spend, to borrow, and to invest based on 60 years of inflation. Deflation will turn all these habits upside down.

As I said before, deflation is not inevitable. The Fed will undoubtedly try to counteract deflationary pressures as they emerge in America. However, it's not at all clear that the Fed will be successful. This chapter is intended to prepare you, and your investment portfolio, for a deflationary environment.

If a hurricane were approaching, most people would prepare themselves in two ways: (1) They would do everything possible to protect their loved ones and their belongings from the ravages of the storm; (2) They would keep a very close eye out to determine whether the storm is likely to hit them with full force or pass them by. Preparing for deflation is like preparing for a financial hurricane.

Our first step is to protect our most important assets from the storm. What assets am I talking about? For each of us the answer could be different. Most Americans probably think of family and home as our most valuable assets. Those of us who don't have a family or a home still have something else important that we want to protect, perhaps a business or a college education fund or an investment portfolio.

Whatever the asset, start protecting it now, before the storm hits. This in very important because the preparation will usually take a long time. If you wait to see the eye of the hurricane before acting, it may well be too late.

Now comes the hard part: To prepare for the storm, many Americans will need to reduce debt. For the average American this is no easy task. It will require time and sacrifice. But the sacrifice is worth it to protect your valuable assets. Debt will be your worst enemy in a period of deflation. If you don't reduce it now, while the economy and the financial markets are relatively healthy, you may well lose control of your assets and your destiny when the storm hits.

Bringing debt under control is undoubtedly the most crucial and difficult task in preparing for deflation. Borrowing has become so ingrained in consumer behavior over the past decades that it will be a tough habit for most Americans to break.

But even those who are disciplined enough to succeed at this, or fortunate enough to have no debt to begin with, have work to do. Structuring your financial assets to weather the deflationary storm is your other task.

The good news here is that restructuring your assets is a lot easier than reducing your debt, and it can be done relatively quickly. However, you'll need to constantly monitor your asset allocation as the storm approaches. Even if we assume that deflation will arrive, we don't know exactly how and when. Most likely it'll last quite a long time. But will it be as severe as what America witnessed in the 1930s, or more mild, as Japan is experiencing today? While I suspect it will be somewhere in between, no one can really answer this question at this point. Just remember that the storm can change directions, and if it does you may need to alter your asset allocation accordingly.

Which assets will perform well in a deflationary environment and which will not? If you remember nothing else from this book, remember this: Bonds are the investment of choice in a deflationary world. Here's why.

In deflation, any asset that can hold its value and deliver a stable stream of income will be attractive. Because bonds promise to redeem a fixed amount of principal at maturity and meanwhile deliver a fixed stream of income, they enjoy a distinct advantage over most other assets during deflationary periods. This is because most other assets like commodities, real estate, and stocks don't promise to repay any fixed amount and have no maturity. In addition, they generally pay out much lower levels of income (as dividends) than bonds. Even those assets that do pay relatively high income, like certain kinds of real estate, may see rental income decline in a very difficult economy.

Obviously, bonds offer a much more predictable return than most other assets. However there's also a psychological aspect that makes bonds attractive in a deflationary world. To fully appreciate why bonds will look good, you need to understand that investors will come to view the future in a much different light than they do today. At the moment investors look to the future with a great deal of hope, anticipating a steady rise in corporate earnings that will lead to higher dividends (income) and eventually higher stock prices. But in a deflationary world investors will look to the future with a great deal of trepidation. Instead of higher corporate earnings and stock prices they will begin to expect lower earnings and stock prices. In short, investors will discount a bleak future as deflation emerges.

As this negative psychology begins to take hold, investors will seek out more conservative investments that pay high current income and guarantee the return of principal. At the same time investors are likely to shun assets that don't offer much income or don't guarantee a return of principal. In this environment bonds come out on top.

Will all bonds be attractive? The answer depends on the severity of the deflation. Bonds come in many different varieties: short-term, long-term, government, corporate, investment grade, junk, and convertible. In an era of mild deflation, all types of bonds may do well. But in a severe deflation accompanied by a sick economy, as we had in the 1930s, the best investments will be medium- to long-term government bonds and very high-quality corporate bonds. Lower-quality bonds, often referred to as junk bonds, are less attractive because they may have difficulty making interest and principal payments. On the other hand, though very short-term bonds that mature in a year or less may be safe, they're not likely to produce a steady flow of income. Interest rates will decline significantly in a deflationary environment. As rates fall, investors will reap less and less income as their bonds mature.

As deflation approaches, the best course of action is to concentrate investment on a diversified portfolio of high-quality bonds that mature in five to ten years. As the severity of the deflationary storm becomes more apparent, you can adjust your portfolio accordingly.

Gold is another asset that might do well (see Figure 8-1). At first this may seem strange, since gold is a commodity, and we know that most commodities fare poorly in periods of deflation. In addition, most investors think of gold as an inflation hedge; if there's no inflation, why hold gold?

Figure 8-1 Gold Prices

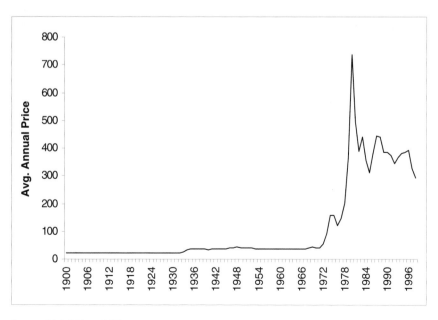

Source: Global Financial Data

Indeed, gold is a very controversial asset class and opinions vary widely as to how it will perform in an era of deflation. Bulls tend to focus on two main points:

1. Gold has generally held its value throughout thousands of years of history, including periods of deflation as well as hyperinflation. The most recent example of this is the Asian economic crisis of 1997-1998, when gold investors throughout Asia fared quite well as stock markets and local currencies collapsed and many corporations went bankrupt. In many cases gold even outperformed high-quality bonds, because capital flight led to plummeting currencies and higher interest rates. The popular press tended to emphasize the role of the U.S. dollar as a safe haven during the Asian crisis, yet gold was another safe haven.

2. In our own experience of the 1930s gold prices and gold stocks rose appreciably in value. But at that time gold prices were still fixed (linked) to the dollar. In 1934 gold prices were revalued upward, from $20 to $35 per ounce, in an effort to effectively devalue the U.S. dollar. Gold stocks naturally soared. Without this action, we can only speculate on how gold would have fared during the Great Depression. Most analysts' opinions on gold tend to track their opinions on the dollar inversely: If they're bullish on the dollar, they're likely to be bearish on gold, and if they're bearish on the dollar, they're likely to be bullish on gold.

My own opinion is that the dollar will become quite weak as the economy and the market begin to fall. This opinion is based on two undeniable facts: First, as noted in chapter 5,we're a nation with a very low savings rate. Second, America runs a very large and growing trade deficit. The result is that, as a nation, we're very dependent on foreign capital. This is acceptable as long as foreigners maintain confidence in our economy. If that confidence begins to erode, as I suspect it will, the dollar can be expected to fall considerably.

Over the past five years the world has witnessed several financial crises spreading across the globe, from Mexico to Asia and Russia, and most recently to Brazil. Except for Russia, all these economies had experienced an economic boom partially fueled by an influx of foreign capital. When problems arose and confidence began to erode, foreign investors quickly withdrew their capital, precipitating a collapse in the domestic currency.

Inevitably after a collapse analysts admonished these countries for being overly dependent on foreign capital—but few analysts warned investors about the vulnerability of these countries before their downfall.

The consensus today is that America, while quite dependent on foreign capital, need not worry about a loss of confidence overseas. Most presume that, as the leading economic power, we're immune to the currency risks associated with Mexico, Brazil, or Asia. But this may be overly optimistic. The dollar's current strength may prove temporary.

History is littered with examples of currencies waxing and waning dramatically. For a time in the 1980s and early 1990s the Japanese yen seemed as invincible as the Japanese economy. The combination of a large trade surplus and high domestic savings seemed to insure a strong yen as far as the eye could see. However, the onset of a weak economy and very low interest rates caused Japanese investors to seek investments beyond their shores. In the late 1990s this movement of funds out of Japan caused the yen to weaken considerably (see Figure 8-2).

Figure 8-2 Japanese Yen to U.S. Dollar

Source: Economagic.com

The U.S. dollar is far more susceptible to weakness than the yen as long as we maintain a low savings rate and a large trade deficit. As long as the U.S. economy is the strongest of the developed economies around the world, the dollar is likely to maintain its strength. However, if our stock market is indeed the bubble it appears to be, it will eventually burst and the U.S. dollar will lose support very quickly.

Where will foreign investors put their money if they lose faith in the dollar? Surely some of it, perhaps most of it, will return to the euro or the yen as investors repatriate their capital. However, a collapse of the U.S. market may well cause investors to lose confidence in the global economy. In this environment, investors across the globe may come to view gold as a prudent alternative to local currency.

This is not to say that investors will put most of their money in gold. However, even a relatively small movement into gold could cause a massive rise in its price. Because very few Americans own gold at the moment, prices are low and gold stocks are very cheap (see Figure 8-3). A collapse in our currency may well ignite a bull market in gold, just as a fall in interest rates propelled the current bull market in stocks. Therefore I recommend that investors establish a small position in gold or high-quality gold stocks, representing approximately 3 to 5 percent of the total portfolio. Once again this position can be adjusted when the storm hits: Depending on the outlook for the dollar, you may then want to increase or decrease your gold position.

Figure 8-3 Gold Index

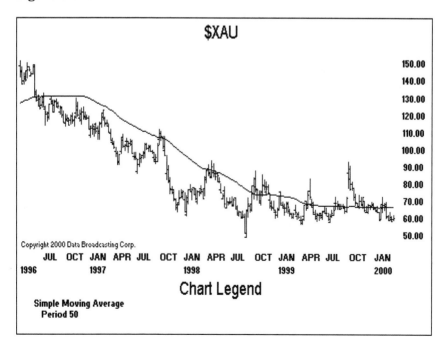

Source: Data Broadcasting Corporation

Now let's examine assets that should be avoided in a deflationary environment. Americans have more money invested in stocks than any other asset class, including equity in their homes. Therefore, the performance of stocks during a deflationary period should be of utmost interest to them.

The news here is sobering. Much has been written recently on the likely performance of stocks in a deflationary period. Some have pointed out that it's possible to experience a benign deflation that is actually favorable to stocks. America witnessed a period like this in the late 1800s (during the industrial revolution) when prices did indeed fall as tremendous increases in productivity led to lower costs and lower prices. Demand stayed strong because prices fell faster than wages, leading to greater levels of purchasing power. Stocks performed reasonably well during this period. While stock prices were not a lot higher in 1895 than they were in 1870, one must remember that any asset class that holds its value during deflation is relatively attractive because other prices are declining.

The great difference between the deflation of the 1930s and that of the late 1800s was in demand. In the 1930s demand collapsed as confidence in the economy began to erode. Some analysts have suggested that our economy may be entering a period of enhanced productivity growth similar to the late 1800s, which will bring with it a benign deflation. In other words, "don't worry, even if deflation arrives demand will hold up and all will be well with the economy and the stock market."

There are some clear reasons to doubt this optimistic scenario. First, as I pointed out in earlier chapters, the 1920s also experienced a great leap in productivity. Yet the tremendous productivity advances of that era didn't prevent the collapse of confidence, and demand, after the crash of 1929. Consumer confidence is the critical factor in demand. Logic, and history, would suggest that productivity alone is not a good predictor of consumer confidence.

Another reason that we should be very suspicious of the optimistic view of deflation is debt. The real cost and burden of debt rises as prices begin to fall. Therefore, consumers and investors will naturally try to reduce debt in a period of deflation. They can accomplish this by selling assets (stocks) and reducing spending.

This fact is absolutely critical to an understanding of deflation. Any attempt to predict the severity, and the consequences, of deflation must consider overall outstanding debt. Currently, total private-sector debt in America is 140 percent of GDP (see chapter 9). In 1928 it was less than 100 percent of GDP.[1] The absence of reliable financial statistics from the late 1800s prevent a detailed comparison with that era. However, the general aversion to debt in pre-World War I America suggests that debt levels in 1878 were far lower than in 1928.[2] The point here is that debt levels have expanded substantially during this century and are now much higher than during prior deflationary eras.

Given the enormous consumer debt burdens today, it's difficult to imagine a benign deflation in America. It's also very hard to believe that stocks will hold up. Current valuations can only be supported by tremendous optimism about future levels of corporate earnings. This optimism is almost sure to erode as deflationary expectations set in. As stock prices fall, America is likely to see the "wealth effect" in reverse: Investors will feel poorer as the value of their stockholdings decline. This will cause them to reduce their spending, further dampening the outlook for the economy and corporate profits.

Deflation will affect the stock market in two ways: First, it will lead to additional price pressures that will cause corporate earnings to

---

[1] *The Economist*, "Could it Happen Again," page 19-22, February 20, 1999.

[2] James Grant, *Money of the Mind,* Noonday Press, 1992.

decline. The extent of this decline will depend on consumer demand. Second, it will lower future expectations, leading to significantly lower P/E ratios.

Let's see how this might affect the market. In June 1999 the S&P 500 was trading at 1,300, or just about 32 times expected earnings of $40. If the market were to trade at a slightly lower, but still historically high, P/E ratio of 25 times earnings, that would put the S&P at about 1,000. In other words it would result in a market drop of almost 30 percent.

Now let's assume that the P/E ratio falls to the middle of its historical range, 15 times earnings. This scenario would result in the S&P going to 600—a drop of over 50 percent.

Keep in mind that a deflationary period like we had in the 1930s or Japan has today would likely result in a precipitous decline in earnings. At our market bottom in 1932, earnings on the Dow were actually negative. Not until 1948 did earnings reach the levels attained in 1929. It's anybody's guess when Japan will return to its earnings peak of 1989, but here we're a decade later and earnings still seem to be declining there. In each of the last three recessions in America (1990, 1982, and 1974), earnings on the Dow declined 25 to 50 percent. A normal recession in America today, accompanied by deflation, could easily cause earnings to drop over 50 percent.

This is not to suggest that all stocks in the U.S. are overpriced and due for a fall. Indeed, some sectors of the market appear reasonably priced by historical standards. But even these stocks may not hold up in the coming bear market.

Investors should pay particular attention to the risks in a couple of areas. First and foremost is the technology sector. Like the Nifty-Fifty stocks of the late 1960s, the tech stocks are clearly the most popular and expensive stocks of the day. When this bull market finally peaks, it could take decades for tech investors to recover their losses.

The other area to be concerned about is companies with a high degree of leverage (debt). These stocks are particularly vulnerable to deflation. Pricing pressures will devastate their earnings. Many will not survive.

The clear message here is that most U.S. stocks are likely to be very poor performers in a period of deflation. Given the potential for deflation, many Americans need to seriously reassess their stock exposure. Unfortunately, history suggests that most will not do so in time. The lure of quick profits will keep many at the party too long. My advice is to begin walking away from the party now, before it's too late. There's an old saying that they don't ring a bell at the top. In other words most investors won't recognize the peak until long after it's passed.

My sense is that many investors today realize that stocks no longer represent good value but they're reluctant to leave the party when it's so much fun. After all, the gain in the market from 1995 through 1999 has been nothing short of spectacular. Over this period the Dow has gained almost 200 percent. This advance is comparable, on a percentage basis, to the one that took place between 1925 and the ultimate top in August of 1929. Another coincidence perhaps? I don't think so. A similar advance took place in the final five years of Japan's bull market, from 1985 to 1989, as the market moved up over 200 percent. Long bull markets have a way of conditioning investors to become even more speculative late in the game, leading to an acceleration of the advance ahead of the final peak.

Please keep in mind that my comments here are directed at the U.S. market only. I don't want to imply that all stock markets are overpriced. A period of worldwide deflation is likely to produce a difficult environment for stock markets everywhere. However, some markets around the world seem already to have discounted a lot of bad news, thereby offering opportunity for long-term investors. The most obvious of these opportunities is Japan.

It may at first seem counterintuitive to begin investing in a country going through a virtual depression. But consider that Japan is currently at about the same stage that the U.S. was in the late 1930s, arguably one of the best times of the century to be accumulating stocks. The Japanese economy is mired in a long slump after peaking almost a decade earlier, interest rates are down to virtually zero, the stock market is bouncing along the bottom of a 10-year bear market (down 70 percent from the high), Japanese investors are loaded with cash, and stocks are cheap. All in all, Japan is a contrarian investor's dream.

While the Japanese market has begun to rise from its 1998 low, valuations remain attractive (see Figure 8-4). P/E ratios are high, but (as explained in chapter 4) this is due to depressed earnings rather than high prices. More important, the Japanese economy is still in the very early stages of an economic rebound, potentially leading to dramatic corporate profit growth in the years ahead.

If you're frightened by the risks of a stagnant Japanese economy, consider what took place in Japan in late 1998: Interest rates more than tripled, moving from 0.6 percent on a 10-year government bond to over 2 percent. This enormous percentage increase in rates had almost no effect on the stock market. The stock market is so out of favor with local investors (sold out) that even a huge rise in rates doesn't bring about significant selling pressure. Any real recovery in the Japanese economy is likely to fuel a tremendous bull market.

Figure 8-4 Nikkei Index

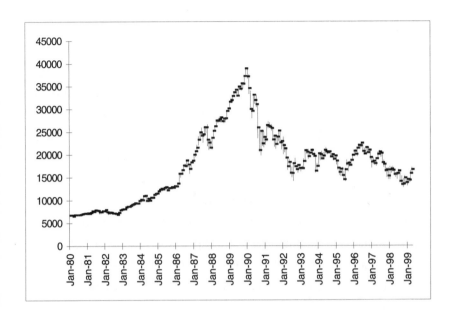

Source: Global Financial Data

Certainly, Japan is not a market for short-term investors. It may well take some time before Japan pulls out of its slump. After all, consumer psychology is still poor, corporate profits are very weak, and deflation has not gone away. However, one very important change has taken place in Japan over the last year or so. That change is the beginning of serious restructuring in corporate Japan. The restructuring comes in many forms, including selling off or merging underperforming assets, eliminating cross-shareholding between friendly corporations, selling stakes to foreign investors to reduce debt or improve efficiencies, and cutting employment to reduce costs.

While these moves may seem commonplace to the average U.S. investor, they are nothing short of revolutionary in Japan. Before long, these restructuring moves should begin to bear fruit in the form of higher corporate profits.

Therefore, for those with a five to 10-year time horizon, I would strongly suggest accumulating Japanese blue chip stocks. One of the easiest ways to do this is to purchase WEBS (World Equity Benchmark Shares). This is nothing more than an index of leading Japanese companies, including most of the stocks in the Nikkei 225 index. The index trades here in the U.S. under the symbol EWJ.

In summary, prepare for a deflationary storm by reducing debt, minimizing exposure to U.S. stocks, maximizing exposure to high-quality bonds, and maintaining a small position in gold or high-quality gold stocks. Investors with long-term horizons may want to invest part of their portfolios in Japan, where deflation has already hit and is fully discounted in share prices.

9

BURSTING THE BUBBLE

The evidence of a speculative bubble in the U.S. stock market is overwhelming. Virtually every valuation tool employed by analysts has reached record levels, even surpassing the speculative extremes of 1929. In spite of the ominous risks in this market, speculative activity continues to rise. Long-term investors are outnumbered by short-term speculators and even day-traders. This speculative binge has been aided by the increasing reliance by institutions on derivative hedging and by individuals on online trading.

The fuel for this mania is not a booming economy or surging corporate profits, as some would have you believe. Rather, it's the growing reliance on debt at both the personal and corporate level that keeps the market moving upward. True, much of this long bull market has been driven by the positive fundamentals of falling rates and rising productivity and profits, but in the last several years the fundamental factors have taken a back seat to speculative considerations. Now, the market is no longer rising due to improving fundamentals. It's rising only due to increased speculation. Current earnings and interest rates cannot support this market without a growing contribution from leveraged speculation.

But leverage can't grow indefinitely. Eventually a breaking point will be reached. Like a rubber band that has been stretched too far, excessive leverage will precipitate a rupture in the stock market—and possibly in the real economy. No one knows where that breaking point is, but history suggests we're getting dangerously close.

Personal debt, as a percentage of disposable income, has reached record levels (see Figure 9-1b). Individuals are simply relying more and more on credit card and home equity debt to finance consumption. Some of this debt is clearly going directly into stock speculation, because margin debt has also reached record levels. At the same time, corporate debt is also reaching new heights (see Figure 9-1c and 9-1d), stretching that rubber band even further. Only time will tell if all this corporate debt has been put to good use, but I suspect that much of it has not. In the last 12 months alone, over $300 billion of corporate cash flow has been used to repurchase stock. Given current valuation levels, that's difficult to justify.

Ironically, the press tends to focus on the declining government debt as a percent of GDP (Figure 9-1e). While this trend is welcome, it clearly does not tell the full story. Overall the debt burden of our society has never been higher (Figure 9-1a).

What this tells us is that our current prosperity is built on increasing amounts of leverage. This is not the foundation for a sound and lasting prosperity. Periods of excessive debt growth generally lead to boom/bust economic cycles. What many see today as an economic miracle of productivity-led growth may prove to be a mirage. Our perceived prosperity may be nothing more than a grand illusion built on speculation and leverage.

Figure 9-1a Total Debt vs GDP

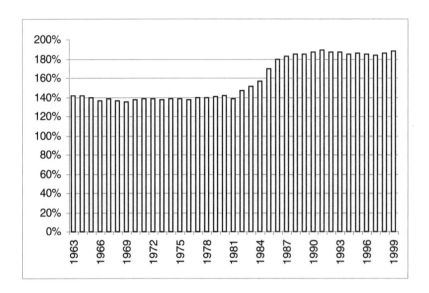

Figure 9-1b Household Debt vs Disposable Personal Income

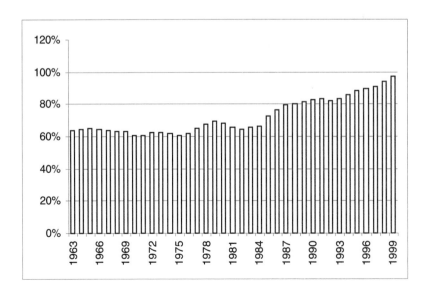

Figure 9-1c Business Debt vs GDP

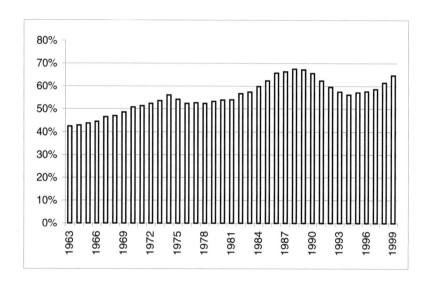

Figure 9-1d Financial Sector Debt vs GDP

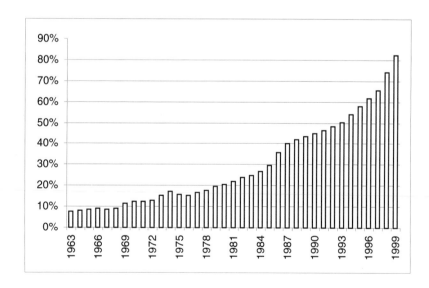

Figure 9-1e Government Debt vs GDP

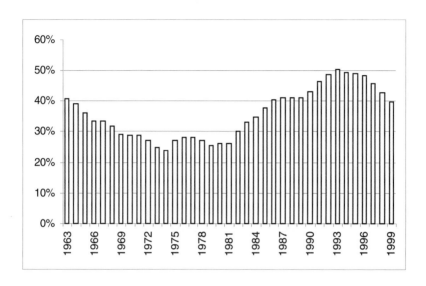

Source: Federal Reserve Statistics

Indeed, the most interesting question before us is not whether we're witnessing a speculative bubble in the U.S. stock market. That seems obvious. The question is how this complex scenario will be resolved in the financial markets and in the real economy. Will the Fed bring this speculative era to an end by raising interest rates? Or will it end of its own accord? How much longer might the good times last? Can we envision the aftermath of this era and predict its severity? These most intriguing questions are the ones I address in this chapter.

First, let's look at the question of longevity: Might this era of debt accumulation and soaring stock prices persist for another five or 10 years, as some have suggested? Or is this bull market in its final days? The answer depends on several factors, including the actions of central bankers and politicians not just in the U.S. but around the world. It will depend on the health of foreign economies, especially the developed economies of Japan and Europe. And it will depend on the behavior of billions of consumers and investors across the globe.

If central bankers continue to provide liquidity and consumers respond optimistically, as they have here in the U.S., then perhaps this era could last several more years. But I suspect the end is much closer at hand. In fact, it may be unfolding before our very eyes, in subtle ways that many fail to recognize.

While it's impossible to predict the behavior of consumers and investors around the globe, there are some important clues we can look for, both here and abroad, that can help us answer the question of longevity. Japan, as the second largest economy and as the biggest creditor to the world, occupies a critical role in the duration of our current prosperity. The huge surplus of Japanese savings exerts an important influence over interest rates and exchange rates around the world. If Japan can generate a lasting consumer-led recovery, then economic growth in Asia should resume. This would relieve some of the tremendous trade imbalances between the U.S. and Asia. It would enable the U.S. to slow consumption a bit without jeopardizing world growth. It would also give the Fed more room, more flexibility, to address the U.S. stock bubble without fear of precipitating a global economic downturn.

Keep in mind that an economic recovery in Japan doesn't mean we can rule out a bear market in U.S. stocks. Indeed, a strong Japanese recovery could well lead to higher interest rates around the world, which could well cause at least a severe correction if not a bear market in the U.S. However, a more gradual economic recovery in Asia could prolong out current bull market. More important, it would reduce the risk of a global deflationary spiral, something we all want to avoid.

Unfortunately, there is as yet no hard evidence of any lasting economic recovery, fast or slow, in Japan. It appears that the Japanese government's massive fiscal stimulus is preventing the economy there from deteriorating. However, it also seems that Japanese consumers remain cautious. For the Japanese recovery to become real and sustainable, the consumer must become much more optimistic.

Japanese government debt has grown dramatically to fund the fiscal stimulus. These budget deficits have been relatively painless so far because of the large surplus of domestic savings. But Japan will find it more and more difficult to expand its fiscal deficits. Eventually economic pressures, in the form of higher interest rates, will limit the government's capacity to borrow. Ultimately, the Japanese consumer must take the pressure off the government if there is to be a lasting recovery.

Meanwhile, in the U.S. there are already signs of trouble in the stock market and in the real economy. One of the most important short-term market indicators is deteriorating badly. The breadth of the market, as depicted in the advance/decline line, measures the cumulative number of net advances (rising issues minus falling issues) in stocks on a daily or weekly basis (see Figure 9-2). A rising advance/decline line means that liquidity is improving, providing a measure of support to the overall market. However, when the advance/decline line is falling, as it has been since April 1998, liquidity is disappearing and the market is becoming more vulnerable (see Figure 9-3).

Figure 9-2a & 9-2b Breadth of the Market Indicators

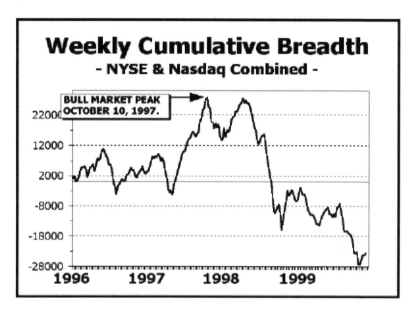

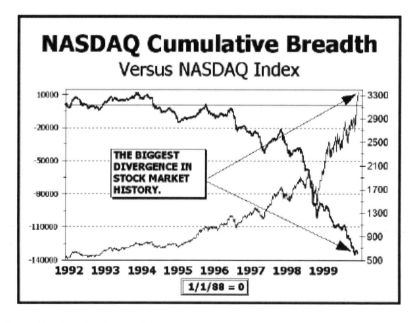

Source: Courtesy of H.D. Brous & Co., Inc.

Figure 9-3 NYSE Market Breadth 1996-1999

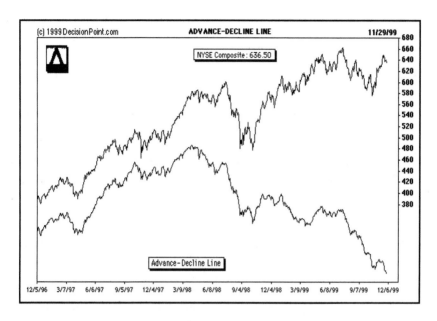

Figure 9-4 Dow Market Breadth 1927-1939

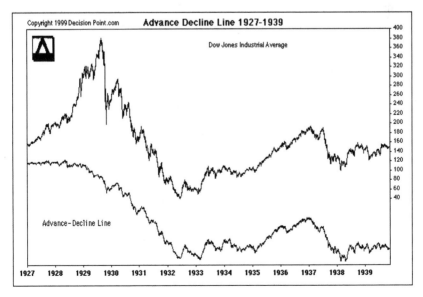

Source: Decision Point.com

Notice in Figure 9-4 how market breadth similarly began to deteriorate in 1928, well ahead of the crash of 1929. Notice also that an overall index (be it the Dow, the S&P, or the NASDAQ) may continue to rise even while the advance/decline line is falling. This occurs as money leaves the average stock to chase a smaller and smaller number of high fliers. This process can produce huge gains in the high fliers, pulling the indexes up even as average stocks are moving lower. Eventually, the falling liquidity catches up with the high fliers, causing the overall market to "correct" (fall).

We cannot be certain about the longevity of this bull market based solely on the advance/decline line. However, throughout history detiorating breadth has proved to be an excellent leading indicator of market tops. The current extended period of deterioration in this indicator has been rivaled only twice in this century. Before the 1973-1974 bear market there was a long period of negative breadth as the average stock lagged behind the speculative surge of the Nifty-Fifty stocks. That period ended when the Dow fell 45 percent. There was also a long period of negative breadth before the crash of 1929 (see Figure 9-4), which culminated in a drop of almost 90 percent. This indicator suggests we should be prepared for an imminent end to this bull market.

As for the real economy, fundamental deterioration is already evident at both the consumer and the corporate level. As shown in chapter 5, personal bankruptcies are approaching record levels, even with very low unemployment and after a very long period of economic growth.

At the corporate level, bond defaults are rising rapidly in spite of the long expansion. In the first six months of 1999, corporate defaults exceeded $20 billion. At this pace, the default rate is running at twice the level experienced during all of 1998. The last time we saw so much distress in corporate finances was during the recession year of 1991.

The only logical reason for these economic distress signals during a period of general prosperity is excessive personal and corporate debt. This debt has been rising for a very long time; it's beginning to take a toll. When the next economic downturn arrives, the U.S. economy is likely to have a whopping hangover from the borrowing binge of the 1990s.

Clearly, both the stock market and the economy signal that all is not well in this supposedly "new era" economy. On the contrary, all the indicators are telling us that risks today are extraordinarily high.

Whenever parallels are made to the 1920s, images of the crash of 1929 and the Great Depression that followed inevitably come to mind. You may wonder if our market and our economy will repeat that scary scenario. Unfortunately, the question is difficult to answer.

The best that market analysts and economists can hope to do is to give you an appraisal of the risks based on the similarities and differences between today and earlier periods. The extreme overvaluation in today's stock market clearly increases the likelihood of a severe bear market decline. But will the market crash suddenly as it did in 1929?

Likewise, the deflationary risks in today's global economy are more pronounced than at any time since the 1930s. But will America experience another Great Depression? No one can answer these questions.

There are reasons to believe that future economic declines will be far less severe than the experience of the Great Depression, when rapid price deflation and unemployment levels of 25 percent caused massive economic and social suffering. Today we have welfare programs to support the unemployed. We have FDIC insurance to protect bank depositors. In short, we have programs in place that are designed to prevent a general collapse of the banking system and to provide economic assistance to those in need. Together these measures should cushion the impact of deflationary forces and help us avoid future depressions.

But we would be wrong to assume that policymakers and regulators have completely immunized us against depressions. Our economy and our financial markets are constantly changing. Just as viruses sometimes mutate and become resistant to vaccines, our economy today may prove resistant to the financial reforms that were designed to vaccinate the economy against severe economic downturns. Many of these reforms were put in place in the 1930s—but the regulations established in the 1930s were created to safeguard a banking and financial system far different from the one we have today.

In the 1920s and 1930s the vast majority of consumer saving and borrowing took place directly through the banks. The Federal Reserve therefore had a great deal of control over money supply growth and credit availability.

Today, our financial system is far more complex. Bank savings accounts represent only a small fraction of our overall savings. All sorts of financial intermediaries help us save and invest; through these, the stock market has become the recipient of most of our savings.

Lending has also changed greatly. Corporations typically go not to banks but to the securities markets (stocks and bonds) when they need to borrow. Individuals also have many more borrowing choices today (e.g., borrowing against 401k plans or from credit card companies).

The result of these changes is that the Fed, while still powerful, does not have the same control over the economy that it once did. Its influence has diminished steadily over the years as our financial system has adapted to include many new savings and lending institutions

Often, we don't fully appreciate the magnitude of these changes, or understand the risks, until something malfunctions. Periodically we're reminded of these risks. The recent collapse of Long-Term Capital was one such reminder. The failure of portfolio insurance during the 1987 crash was another. In both cases, the widespread use of derivatives gave investors a false sense of security. It was assumed that positions were hedged to prevent large losses. In both cases, investors miscalculated: The hedges didn't work as expected, losses mushroomed and the consequences were severe. When Long-Term Capital collapsed, our financial system was very nearly brought to its knees.

Can this happen again? Absolutely. And very likely it will happen again. The question is where and when.

Often, financial crises are caused by periods of excessive lending. In the 1970s, international banks were flush with petrodollar deposits from the Middle East. They lent much of this money to the developing countries on the assumption that no country would default on its sovereign debt.

In the 1980s we learned that even countries can become insolvent. The result of this excessive lending was a debt crisis that very nearly bankrupted all of South America.

After the Latin crisis most U.S. banks decided that lending at home was safer than lending abroad. Much of that lending went to finance real estate, presumed to be an asset class that would never decline in value. In the early 1990s we learned that even real estate loans can go sour. In the process we nearly suffered a collapse of our banking system.

The interesting thing about these episodes is that the problems arose in those areas where banks seemed most anxious to lend. In other words, our banking industry does not seem very good at recognizing risks in the macro-economy brought on by excessive lending. Part of the problem is that some banks don't see the risks. They simply misjudge the creditworthiness of the borrower. However, it's hard to imagine that most banks simply are ignorant of credit excesses as they develop.

Most likely, banks perceive the growing risks but feel that the high profits more than compensate for the risks: The long-term risks are overshadowed by the short-term profit projections. The basic problem here is that profit margins in the banking industry are not actually known until the loans are repaid, which could be several years or even decades down the road. In the meantime, banks record "profits" based on assumed margins. If banks systematically underestimate the risks certain borrowers pose, by definition they're overestimating the margins and profitability (if any) of that business. When banks extend large amounts of credit to a certain class of borrowers who prove to be unworthy, the system as a whole may be put at risk.

The purpose of this analysis is not to suggest that bankers are solely to blame for our past, or any future, banking crises. Surely borrowers must accept at least as much blame as the lenders. Rather, I'm suggesting that we should be able to anticipate potential risks to our system by analyzing areas of excessive credit growth.

In today's economy, credit excesses appear most prevalent in the consumer lending arena. Over the last decade, banks have loaned money to individuals very aggressively via credit cards and home equity loans. It seems almost absurd how easy it can be to borrow money in our society. Just open your mailbox or log onto the Internet and you're likely to be bombarded with credit offers.

The long economic expansion of the 1990s may have convinced banks that consumer loans have very little risk. At the same time, the good economy may have convinced most consumers (borrowers) that they can handle their growing credit card (and home equity) burdens.

I have my doubts. Just as long bull markets lead investors to underestimate the risks of stocks, long economic expansions lead consumers to be overly optimistic about their finances.

My guess is that the next banking crisis will be right here at home in the form of consumer debt defaults. It should show up when the next bear market arrives.

Will the banking system collapse? Will we have a depression? Fortunately these scenarios are unlikely. But we could experience a long period of economic distress, much like Japan's in the 1990s. The years ahead may not be nearly as dramatic as the depression years of the 1930s, but they could be very unsettling for those Americans who now take a healthy economy for granted.

As this depressing economic scenario unfolds, many Americans will become angry. They may well vent their frustrations on corporate and government leaders. The most likely scapegoat in this situation is the chairman of the Federal Reserve, Alan Greenspan. This is truly ironic, because Greenspan has been diligently warning the American public about the dangers of reckless stock speculation and excessive credit for over three years now.

While I have a great deal of respect and admiration for Greenspan, there is one question that troubles me: If he was so concerned about the asset bubble in the stock market, why didn't he act to deflate it earlier? Clearly his remarks about "irrational exuberance" in late 1996 were designed to do just that. But when those remarks had no effect on the market, why didn't he take more concrete steps to prevent the bubble from becoming even larger? I've pondered this question many times.

Essentially, Greenspan had two options, two tactics he could have used to deflate the bubble. One option would be to raise interest rates, which would divert the flow of money away from stocks and into bonds. However, this would also have slowed the real economy, which was not his aim in 1996. The real economy seemed to be growing at a desirable pace, with very little inflation. Raising rates might have jeopardized our economic expansion and risked stimulating deflationary pressures.

Actually some economists would argue that we did experience considerable inflation in the 1990s. The inflation, they contend, took the form of higher prices for financial assets, primarily stocks and bonds. They would also argue that "asset price" inflation poses a risk to the economy that equals the more traditional "goods"-based inflation the CPI measures.

The debate over the definition of inflation may not be new, but it seems more relevant as stocks reach unprecedented valuations. In any case, it's an issue for another book. What should be clear to you, however, is that the 1990s were very similar to the 1920s in that stock prices soared while "traditional" inflation was almost nonexistent.

The other option available to Greenspan was to leave interest rates alone while raising the margin requirements on stocks. This course of action seems far more logical since it attacks the real problem, excessive stock prices, while leaving the real economy alone. I believe this would have been the correct policy for the Fed to take in 1997. In sending a clear message to investors, it might have prevented the day-trading mania from taking hold.

Certainly, Greenspan must have considered both of these options as he deliberated how to deal with the irrational exuberance overtaking America. His decision to leave interest rates alone may be entirely understandable, given the economic circumstances at the time, but his complete lack of response to the growing asset bubble remains a mystery. Clearly, Greenspan has been very concerned about the stock market, for he has spoken of this problem virtually every time he appeared in public from late 1996 on. Yet he chose not to act until inflation finally showed up in the CPI in 1999, at which time he began to raise interest rates.

Mr. Greenspan addressed the margin requirement issue publicly, stating that it would be unfair to the small investor if the Fed were to raise margin requirements. But surely that course of action is more equitable than the alternative: raising interest rates that hurt all investors (including those not using margin) and consumers.

My guess is that Greenspan's actions (or lack thereof) were guided by his strong philosophical opposition to government intrusion on the free market. This outlook is consistent with most of the decisions he has made while at the helm of the Fed. For instance, after the Long-Term Capital crisis Greenspan testified that he would be opposed to government regulation of hedge funds or the use of derivatives. He clearly recognized the risks to the financial system posed by hedge funds that employ excessive leverage. He also knows that derivatives play a key role in this leverage. Yet he felt those risks were outweighed by the beneficial role that derivatives play in reducing risk for many market participants.

Greenspan has exceptional faith in our free market system. In his view, government obtrusion into the market is more likely to aggravate the problem rather than resolve it. Judging by his actions, he seems to feel that the Fed's overriding mission is to foster price stability. Only the clear presence of inflationary or deflationary price trends warrants Fed intervention, in his view. All other problems should be left for the free market to resolve.

I suspect that Greenspan's main concern is that the current stock market bubble will implode into a deflationary spiral. He knows that fighting deflation is every bit as difficult as fighting inflation. In any case, Greenspan has, until recently, chosen to combat the bubble with words rather than actions. So far, there seems to be little evidence that his strategy is working.

Regardless of the ultimate outcome of this economic drama, Greenspan's position is not enviable. If the bull market ends of its own accord, many will come forward to criticize him for not dealing with the bubble earlier. Yet if he acts to deflate the bubble by raising interest rates or margin requirements, others will blame him for precipitating the stock market decline.

CHAPTER

10

CONCLUSION

For some time now, I've been aware of the fascinating financial and economic parallels between the 1920s and the 1990s. But interest rate trends, stock market valuations, and other economic statistics can never tell the whole story. I've always believed that psychology plays a crucial role in economic and market risks. Over the last 17 years, I've seen tremendous psychological changes in the investing habits of my clients. In observing these changes I've come to realize that we are indeed witnessing a rare period in the history of American financial markets.

When I came into this business in 1983, stocks were very cheap, interest rates were declining and the economy was emerging from a serious recession. The Dow had just broken out of a 17-year trading range, exploding above 1,000 on record volume. In short, all signs indicated that we were embarking on a new bull market with tremendous upside potential.

As I endeavored to communicate this bullish message to clients, I quickly realized that most investors had a different view of the financial markets. While I was focused on the potential of what lay ahead, most were focused on the reality of the past.

The 1970s were a lousy decade for the stock market. Inflation had propelled hard assets like real estate, oil, and precious metals substantially higher, while most stocks and bonds languished. Investors came to believe that paper assets (stocks and bonds) held little appeal. In 1983 very few people believed that inflation and interest rates would decline for an extended period of time to the benefit of financial assets. Thus few were willing to take the plunge into stocks or equity mutual funds in spite of some very promising fundamental trends.

It was this sobering experience that led me to realize that past performance has a far more profound impact on investor psychology and expectations than any fundamental considerations. This simple fact has never been more evident than it is today, when the Dow stands above 10,000, having risen more than tenfold since the beginning of this bull market in 1982. Stock valuations are exorbitant by any rational measure. The signs of exuberance normally associated with market tops are everywhere. The number of investment clubs, mutual funds, and investment analysts has exploded. Mergers and acquisitions have reached record levels.

Many books exposing the virtues of the stock market have become bestsellers. One such book chronicled the activities of an investment club know as the Beardstown Ladies. These women were apparently quite successful in the market, employing little more than patience and common sense. (Subsequently it was discovered that the investment returns generated by this club were vastly overstated, approximating 10 percent a year rather than the 20 percent-plus returns indicated in the book). More recently, books have appeared with titles of *Dow 20,000*, *Dow 36,000*, and even *Dow 100,000*!

Several TV channels monitor the stock and bond markets all day long, minute by minute. One channel even follows the performance of high school investment clubs, seeming to suggest that we have something to learn from the investment prowess of our young children. The not so subtle message is that investing in stocks is easy and it's for everyone, young and old, experienced or otherwise.

In recent years a new beast in financial markets has emerged. This is the day-trader. Rather than holding stocks for many years, these people hold stocks for minutes or hours. This new breed of "investor" has a completely different attitude from that of more traditional investors. While they may admire the success of long-term investors like Peter Lynch or Warren Buffett, day traders believe that investment success can be achieved much more quickly. As a result, they're impatient with a traditional buy and hold strategy. Many of these day-traders have indeed been very successful in the past three or four years, riding the wave of this incredible bull market. In fact, this success has led many people across the nation to quit their jobs in pursuit of day-trading "careers".

Many day-traders believe they've discovered a simple formula for investment success, aided by advances in technology. What they fail to understand is that they're repeating one of the oldest and most common mistakes in the investment business: confusing a bull market with brains. The dominant strategy employed by most of today's day-traders is to ride the upward momentum of technology stocks. As I've said before, this strategy of buying dips has worked very well lately. Unfortunately these "investors" are doomed to failure unless they're smart enough to abandon this strategy before the next bear arrives. History suggests that very few will be so lucky.

Ultimately, day-trading stocks is a lot like going to the racetrack or the casino. It can be a lot of fun while you're on a hot streak, but those streaks always come to an end. Those who keep playing the game are very likely to become long-term losers. In the end, day-trading will be viewed as pure electronic speculation, not very different from other forms of gambling.

In spite of all the clear signs of speculative excess in today's market, the average American has never been more inclined to venture in the stock market with his/her savings. Clearly, investors are now looking back at the reality of the last decade rather than forward to the risks that lie ahead. Emboldened by 18 years of a powerful bull market, most investors assume that all corrections are buying opportunities, regardless of valuations or other fundamental concerns. Most Americans have indeed become "believers" in the market. Cautious advisors (those few who are left) are generally ignored. Most are afraid to speak out, question valuations, and be laughed at as hopelessly out of date with new-era thinking.

Much of the optimism today is based on a profound faith in the power of demographics. Over and over, the bullish mantra can be heard: "Baby boomers have to save for retirement. What else are they going to do with their money but invest in stocks? Mutual funds will continue to attract cash and this will support the market."

What these investors forget is that there was an explosion of mutual fund activity in the previous bull markets in this century, yet it didn't prevent the inevitable bear market. In the "roaring twenties," mutual funds were referred to as investment trusts. They were bought for their performance, diversification, and perceived safety-just as they are today. In the "go-go sixties," the mutual fund industry once again experienced a period of explosive growth, powered by the public appetite for the market. In the 1980s Japan also saw a surge in mutual fund activity as the Japanese public looked to benefit from the growth of the seemingly invincible Japanese economy.

Figure 10-1 Mutual Funds Assets 1954-1874

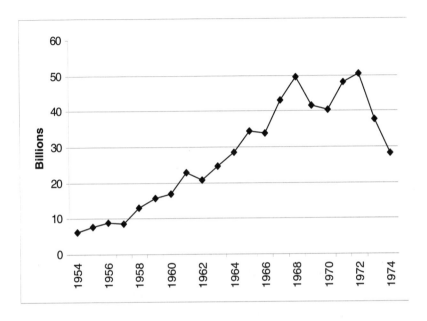

In all these cases, mutual funds proved to be only a temporary attraction to ordinary investors, lured by years of a strong bull market. Ultimately these periods of strong growth ended in a similar, predictable, fashion: As the public lost faith in the market, they abandoned mutual funds as quickly as they had embraced them. In the decades after each of these great bull markets, the fund industry shrank along with public appetite for the market. Many funds became so small that they were no longer profitable to operate; of the six best-performing funds in 1968, all but one had closed up shop before the bear market finally bottomed in 1974 (see Figure 10-1).

Mutual funds are an outgrowth of all great bull markets, but they're a *symptom* of bull markets, not a cause. Today, as in the 1920s and again in the 1960s, many investors believe that funds are so large and powerful that they'll prevent any serious bear market. This faith is bound, once again, to be shattered.

People don't intentionally act irrationally, of course. When markets become so expensive that they can no longer be justified by traditional analysis, many investors seek out new justifications for their profitable speculation. Today many investors have found that justification in demographics. Popular books promote the simple and apparently logical idea that aging baby boomers will fuel this bull market for another decade as they "save" for retirement. The possibility that other forms of saving, such as money markets or bonds, may become popular at the expense of stocks doesn't clutter the minds of these bullish advisors.

But consider the situation today in Japan, whose population is about 10 years older than ours. The Japanese public is indeed saving a great deal of money, but those savings are not going into the stock market. Instead, savings are accumulating in safe bank accounts and government bonds, pushing interest rates extremely low. Though interest rates are well below 1 percent, the Japanese public appears to have little interest in the stock market. The bear market that began in 1990, pulling the market down 70 percent, is still fresh in the minds of most Japanese. It will be some time before the average Japanese citizen regains faith in the stock market. As a generation of Americans learned 70 years ago in 1929, the Japanese have recently learned that the stock market has risks that sometimes overwhelm its potential rewards.

The Japanese situation has some pretty clear messages for investors who are not blinded by optimism. The first is that an aging population may choose not to invest in the stock market, no matter how disciplined its members are about saving for retirement. Negative psychology can keep investors out of the market for a long time.

The other message is one that appears again and again in the history of financial markets: Valuations do matter! For a time giddy investors may ignore high valuations, believing that valuation has somehow lost its relevance in a rapidly changing world. Ultimately, though, excessive valuations will evaporate and the market will retreat to levels that reflect a less optimistic outlook. The risk of this occurring today in the U.S. is extraordinarily high.

There is no question that the spending and saving habits of baby boomers will continue to impact our economy and the market in a significant way. Nonetheless investors should be skeptical when they're given an extremely simple explanation for an extremely complex phenomenon. The behavior of the stock market has frustrated and confused experts for centuries. Many very sharp minds have tried to unlock the formula that can accurately predict the direction of the market. All of these efforts have met with only limited success.

The stock market is simply a giant discounting mechanism that incorporates the opinions and emotions of millions of investors throughout the world. These opinions are based on predictions of future interest rates and corporate earnings, economic growth rates, consumer sentiment readings, government policy initiatives, and hundreds of other factors, only one of which is demographics. From time to time investors may become focused on the predictive value of one factor above all others. In the early 1980s, for instance, investors were riveted to the weekly money supply figures, believing they were the key to future inflation and interest rate movements. Eventually, as that conviction began to wane, investors turned their attention on other factors. Today, money supply figures are mostly ignored by the financial press and the investment community.

The spending and saving habits of baby boomers are certainly relevant factors to consider in anticipating future interest rates and stock prices. But to believe that demographics alone can determine the course of the market is pure nonsense. Five years from now, I suspect most investors will have forgotten about demographics as a predictive tool, just as they lost interest in money supply figures.

My concerns about the current environment are based on both objective and subjective observations. The objective concerns relate to the tremendous overvaluation documented in chapter 4. The subjective concerns emanate from my interactions with many ordinary investors since 1983. Over this period I've learned a thing or two about investor behavior.

One of the first things you learn as a financial advisor is that most investors are emotional and impatient. They may claim to be long-term investors who understand stock market volatility, but at the first sign of a downturn, their emotions start to affect their thinking. Often they begin to act like short-term traders. The average investor today can tolerate a quarter or two of negative returns without losing that long-term focus. However, given a year or more of negative returns, most investors begin to lose faith in the long-term potential of stocks. In a true bear market, where stocks drop 20 percent or more and stay down for over a year, investor psychology will turn decidedly negative.

Today's investors will not sit through a prolonged bear market with their psyche intact. Many will become so emotional that they will sell in order to reduce their anxiety. Many will simply freeze, anxious to get out of the market but unwilling to take a loss. A very small number will view the decline as an opportunity to accumulate stocks for the long haul. Given today's record overvaluation, I expect the next bear market will test investor psychology as never before.

The most disturbing trend that I've noticed in recent years is the growing tendency of extremely conservative but inexperienced investors to become shareholders. These people have not come into the market with realistic risk/return expectations. Most fail to understand that, over the long run, the market only rewards investors who have the patience and discipline to stay the course during turbulent times.

These conservative investors have gravitated towards the stock market in recent years for a couple of reasons: First, the unprecedented strength and duration of this bull market has led many younger investors to conclude that the stock market is the only logical place to put their money. Many of these individuals have seen friends, neighbors, and relatives make a great deal of money in the market over the last five to ten years. More and more of these conservative investors are asking themselves, "Why don't I participate in this?" Many have decided to take the plunge.

There's another class of conservative investors who tend to be much older. These investors have moved into stocks out of fear rather than greed. They've traditionally put their money in bonds or CDs; from the late 1970s to the early 1990s, this strategy produced relatively high rates of return with relatively little risk. But with rates moving progressively lower, it's becoming more and more apparent to these investors that high rates of return in the bond market are a thing of the past. They now realize that only through the stock market can they hope to earn the types of returns that they've come to expect. Many of these investors are afraid that if they don't participate in the stock market, their investment returns will decline and they'll be forced to accept a lower quality of life during retirement.

The important point here is that we now have a very large group of conservative and inexperienced investors in the market. We needn't worry about them as long as the market continues to rise. But how will these investors behave when the next bear market arrives? This is a rhetorical question: These investors don't really understand the risk of the market. During the next real bear market, they'll recognize this fact. They'll sell.

No one knows for sure how much their selling will affect the over-all market. There's no objective way to quantify this risk. What I can say is that over the last several years I have observed an unusually large number of investors venturing into the stock market for the wrong reasons. Often they're pursuing short-term gains without regard for valuations or other long-term considerations. This type of behav-ior is typical of the late stages of all investment manias. I'm quite cer-tain that my experience is not unique. Virtually all the seasoned invest-ment advisors that I've spoken with have similar concerns.

Of course, bulls will argue that there's simply no hard evidence to support this pessimistic view. They'll point out that recent history sug-gests that investors are much more patient and rational than I've sug-gested. Though I sincerely hope that the bulls are correct, every day I witness investment behavior that convinces me they're wrong. Investors are pouring record amounts of money into the most overval-ued market of the century, steadfastly ignoring the warnings of Alan Greenspan, Warren Buffet, and George Soros. Is that rational behavior?

This book has focused its attention on the combined risks of an extraordinarily overvalued stock market and a highly leveraged econ-omy. It has attempted to explain why deflation is the most likely out-come of this economic scenario. My objective has been to make you aware of these risks and explain them as clearly as I possibly can. Yet I wouldn't want you to think that the American economy is devoid of positive forces. Forecasting the direction of the economy and the mar-ket is extremely difficult precisely because there are *always* positive and negative trends at work simultaneously.

One of the positive elements in today's environment is the gov-ernment budget surplus. For many years the U.S. government ran a budget deficit, requiring additional borrowing to finance the deficit. Fortunately, this is no longer the case. As a result, the government is borrowing less, interest rates are lower, and the U.S. dollar is stronger. All of these are healthy developments for the U.S. economy.

Another positive factor is the preponderance of just-in-time inventory management. The proliferation of computer technology in today's world has allowed many industries to keep better track of changes in demand. Improved inventory management seems to be reducing the inventory imbalances that were so common in prior economic cycles. Hopefully, this will reduce the severity and length of future economic downturns.

Another recent development that I think may be positive is the increasing incidence of cross-border mergers and acquisitions, such as Daimler-Chrysler and Renault-Nissan. While it's still too early to predict the ultimate duration, extent, and impact of this trend, some potential benefits are already apparent. By facilitating the closure of older, more inefficient production facilities around the globe, these mergers will hopefully reduce the excess capacity that exists in many industries. This will improve overall productivity, increase corporate profitability, and, most importantly, dilute the strength of the global deflationary pressures that emanate from excess capacity.

If this trend continues, we should begin to see a profound impact on workers and shareholders. Gradually, the boundaries between peoples of different homelands should begin to fade. Nationalistic priorities will become more difficult to define. Hopefully, the world will move closer together. When confronted with economic difficulties, perhaps we'll seek to resolve our problems though international cooperation rather than isolationist solutions like barriers to trade. If the world continues to move in this direction, there's hope that we can avoid the destructive force of protectionism that so doomed our economy in the 1930s.

We can be encouraged by these positive developments and we should do everything possible to promote these trends. Yet we shouldn't dismiss the overriding risks that threaten our current prosperity. History strongly suggests that the U.S. economy is on a dangerous path, one dominated by excessive leverage and reckless speculation. If we hope to attain our optimistic view of the future, we'll need to overcome some extraordinary risks in the years ahead.

Appendix

BULL/BEAR CYCLES OF THE TWENTIETH CENTURY

There's no precise definition of what constitutes the beginning or end of a bull market. Bear markets are generally defined as a market drop of 20 percent or more. But over how long, and in what index? Analysts arrive at slightly different interpretations of market cycles depending on their point of view. For our purposes, let's define bull markets as periods of generally rising stock prices as evidenced by major market indices such as the S&P 500 or the Dow, and bear markets as market corrections of 20 percent or more in the major indices.

With these definitions in mind, most analysts will agree that there was three major bull markets and two major bear markets in the U.S. in the twentieth century. The bull cycles were 1921-1929, 1949-1965 and 1982-?. The bear markets were 1929-1932 and 1973-1974.

In looking at these previous cycles it's immediately clear that the bull/bear cycle of the 1920s and 1930s was very different, and quite a bit more dramatic, than the next cycle, which began in 1949. The 1920s/1930s cycle is also somewhat easier to analyze, because the bull market was followed immediately by a devastating bear market. It's pretty clear that the bull cycle ended decisively in 1929!

The end of the 1960s bull market, on the other hand, is far more murky. After the Dow peaked in 1965 at 1,000, the market suffered a series of increasingly severe corrections/bear markets, culminating in the 1973-1974 decline.

The final bull market of the century, which began in 1982, also followed a somewhat peculiar pattern. It included a crash/bear market in 1987 that turned out to be a temporary interruption of the greatest bull market of the century.

Clearly all bull/bear cycles don't follow the same pattern. However, most bull markets do share common characteristics. In fact, it's fascinating to observe how investor behavior often follows similar paths in completely different eras. By comparing the characteristics of the current bull market with those of prior eras, perhaps we can gain some insight into the next inevitable down market.

Almost all bull markets are born in periods of adversity. In fact, all three of the major bull cycles of the past century began during economic recessions. The adversity need not be limited to economic difficulties; often political or social problems accompany them. Typically wars or recessions have wreaked havoc with consumer confidence and investor psychology, leading to falling stock prices and very low market valuations. Then, at some point during these difficult periods, investor psychology begins to turn more positive. Usually, there's a catalyst for this change. It might be a fall in interest rates or a change in political leadership. Sometimes it's simply the realization that economic conditions have stabilized after a long decline. At this point, savvy investors realize that the combination of low stock prices and improving psychology has created opportunity and begin to commit capital to the market. Voila! A bull market is born.

Of course, it's always easier to analyze these turning points in hindsight than to recognize them as they occur. For this reason, most investors don't begin to participate in bull markets until the uptrend is well in place and economic conditions have strengthened. By this time consumer confidence and investor psychology have improved markedly. Stock prices are no longer as cheap as they had been, but investors now feel more comfortable putting their money into the market. They're more confident about the economy and their own financial position.

During the middle stages of a bull market the advance is generally supported by strong economic fundamentals. Interest rates are generally low and perhaps falling, productivity is probably increasing, and consumer demand is strong enough to produce rising corporate profits. At this stage, it seems entirely logical for investors to increase their exposure to the market.

As the bull market ages, valuations continue to rise, as do risks, but most investors don't see the risks. The long bull market has attracted many unsophisticated investors who don't understand valuations. Other, more experienced, investors may recognize the expensive valuations but many have become addicted to the easy money created by the long bull market. Often the economy is so strong that investors have a hard time envisioning a bear market or a recession.

While the economy is virtually always strong at this stage, investment fundamentals usually begin to deteriorate. The pace of corporate profit growth may slow for several different reasons; Interest rates may be rising. Wages may be increasing, leading to smaller increases in productivity. Prudent cost cuts may be harder to come by. Consumer demand, while still healthy, may no longer be increasing at the same rate.

Typically, corporations respond to slower profit growth by engaging in various forms of corporate restructuring. These may include large stock buybacks or aggressive corporate mergers and acquisitions. Inevitably some companies resort to accounting gimmickry to try to hide the fact that core profit growth is beginning to deteriorate.

Surprisingly, this weakening fundamental picture often will not slow the stock market advance. By this stage of the bull market, investor confidence is so strong that apparent problems are rationalized as temporary setbacks to be overlooked. As the stock market continues to advance faster than corporate profits, P/E ratios and other valuation measures rise to unsustainable or irrational levels.

Inevitably, during the final act of long bull markets, the dominant aspect in investor psychology begins to change from confidence to greed. Sound, logical investment analysis gives way to pure speculation. As the sexiest stocks reach astronomical valuation levels, investors begin to believe they must own these stocks at any level. Usually these hot stocks are associated with a new technology that's expected to transform our economy or our society. Near the end of most bull markets, these favorite stocks will carry the market indices higher even while most stocks stagnate or enter corrections.

Speculation shows up in other ways as well. The initial public offering (IPO) market usually heats up at this stage as companies look to cash in on the sky-high prices. Margin debt, too, usually increases as investors, both individuals and corporations, borrow to buy stocks. Of course, some bull markets experience much more speculation than others. There is no precise formula to predict how confident or how irrational investors might become. But all great bull markets witness some or all of these speculative signs.

Eventually, the psychology begins to change. It may be a sudden change that leads to a crash, as happened in 1929 and 1987. Or it may be a more gradual change that leads to a long-drawn-out decline. Once again there's usually a catalyst that brings the bull market to an end. Often, rising interest rates will play a role in this psychological shift.

A rate rise may be a natural outcome of an over-heating economy or it may be an intentional move by the central bank to reign in inflation. In any case, it's very common to witness rising rates as bull markets come to an end.

At this stage experienced investors will recognize the clear signs of excess and begin to reduce their exposure to the market. However, most investors are so convinced of the market uptrend that they're slow to recognize the growing risks. Most market observers will at first assume that any market correction represents a buying opportunity. Then, gradually, as the rallies shorten and the corrections lengthen, more investors come to realize that the bull is no longer on the field.

By this stage the market has probably had a significant drop of at least 20 percent and signs of other economic problems may be surfacing. Consumer and investor confidence is eroding. Stocks are no longer the hot topic of conversation at cocktail parties. Investors now face the difficult decision of selling to prevent further losses or sitting tight and hoping that a bottom is near.

As the bear market progresses, it's very common to see sharp periodic rallies. These are sometimes referred to as "bear traps." The intensity of these rallies is enough to convince some investors that the bear market has ended. Unfortunately, these rallies end quickly, giving investors very little time to exit the market before the bear phase resumes. Timing the end of a bear market is no easier that identifying the top of a bull market Only in hindsight is it obvious.

Near the end of most bear markets we typically witness a capitulation, a "wash-out" phase. At this point the economy is clearly weak and corporate profits are falling. The psychological pressure to sell is intense even though stocks are now very cheap on most valuation measures. Some savvy investors are beginning to anticipate a market bottom but the majority of investors are selling, seeing no hope of a rebound. The market decline usually accelerates now until the selling pressure has exhausted itself. The bull/bear cycle is now complete.

CYCLE #1 : 1921-1932

The years leading up to the 1920s bull market were very difficult indeed. The devastation of World War I and the terror of the Spanish flu epidemic of 1918 were still fresh in people's minds. The economy was in recession in 1920-1921. All in all, these were the most trying of times. As you can imagine, consumer and investor confidence was extremely low.

Then in 1921 a ray of economic hope appeared, in the form of falling interest rates. This was the spark that ignited the bull market of the 1920s. At the market bottom in 1921 the Dow was trading at 65, roughly 1.3 times book value and 16 times dividends. Over the next eight years, the market would experience a meteoric rise led by the great growth companies of that era (see figure A-1). Foremost among these were the automobile companies like General Motors and Ford and the communication companies like Radio Corp of America (RCA) and American Telephone and Telegraph (AT&T).

Consumer and investor confidence surged throughout the 1920s as the tremendous productivity growth of that era led to strong corporate profit growth with low inflation. Disinflation was firmly entrenched in the economy during that decade, pushing interest rates steadily down. Even as the Dow surged ahead from 1927 through 1929, inflation as measured by the CPI was nonexistent.

In virtually every respect, the economy of the 1920s was excellent. America was a strong exporting nation with a large trade surplus and a strong currency. By the end of the decade America had emerged as the world's leading creditor and economic power. The prosperity that it created was funneled into the stock market and other investments, such as real estate. (In fact, there was a boom in Florida real estate until 1926, when a devastating hurricane hit southern Florida.) The bond market also attracted investment but interest rates were quite low. By the late 1920s nothing could compete with the returns being generated in the stock market.

Figure A-1 Dow Jones 1921–1932

Source: Global Financial Data

As you can imagine, investors had every reason to be bullish about the future of the economy and the stock market. New technologies were leading to tremendous increases in productivity and whole new industries were being created, spurred by the spread of electricity across the nation and by the impact of the automobile industry. There was also a growing faith in the ability of the government to control economic cycles with the help of the Federal Reserve Board, which had been created in 1913.

Unfortunately, the undeniable prosperity of the twenties led to a speculative stock market surge, fueled by increasing confidence and low (10 percent) margin requirements. By 1929 margin debt and valuation measures had reached historic proportions. Speculation was also increasing in other areas: Consumers were taking on more debt to buy automobiles and household appliances. Credit was more plentiful than ever and consumers were taking advantage of it.

At the market peak in 1929 the Dow had reached 386, having risen almost six times in the span of eight years. At this level the Dow was trading at over four times book value and about 30 times dividends. The Dow would not approach these valuation levels again until the mid-1960s.

What caused the market to crash in 1929? Clearly, high levels of margin debt played a role in the severity of the decline because over-leveraged investors were forced to sell as the market dropped. Interest rates also could be cited as a reason: The Fed had begun to raise rates in 1928 to cool speculation in the stock market. However, there was no sharp rise in rates on high-quality debt (government bonds and AAA corporate bonds) in 1929. The only real sign of trouble just before the crash was a spike in broker call rates (loans to brokers collateralized by stocks and bonds) to 20 percent early in the year. This caused the Dow to correct from 320 to 280 in March 1929. But one last burst of speculation then carried the Dow up 100 points, almost 40 percent, to its final peak in September 1929.

So there is no simple answer to explain the crash of 1929. All we can say for sure is that high valuations, leveraged speculation, and rising rates all seemed to play a role. The ensuing bear market would erase all the gains of the great bull market, and then some!

The bear market of 1929-1932 would prove to be the worst this country has ever seen. At the market bottom in the summer of 1932, the Dow had fallen all the way from 386 to 40. At these levels the Dow was less than 10 times dividends and about half of book value. Altogether the Dow had dropped almost 90 percent. It would take 25 years for the Dow to recover those losses.

Even after the crash, few investors expected the slump to be prolonged. However, America would soon face a series of other financial and economic setbacks that would devastate consumer confidence. While it's impossible to "blame" the Depression on any one factor, it's quite clear that bank failures played a crucial role in the collapse of consumer confidence. The stock market crash may have impaired the confidence of the wealthy, but most average Americans had no direct exposure to the stock market in 1929. The bank failures, on the other hand, touched almost every American. Consumer confidence plunged once America lost faith in the banking system.

Another critical factor in the economic collapse of the Depression was the Hawley-Smoot tariff, enacted in 1930. This law was originally intended to protect American farmers, who were not doing well economically. The idea was to shield them from low-priced imports by imposing high duties (taxes). However, the law was viewed with alarm by other countries (and some U.S. economists) and soon provoked retaliation. As barriers to trade went up around the world, economic conditions worsened even further.

It's also important to keep in mind that the Depression was a worldwide economic collapse, not just a domestic one. Stock market crashes and banking failures occurred throughout the world. Under these circumstances, it's perhaps not so surprising that the Dow fell 90 percent between 1929 and 1932!

CYCLE #2 : 1949-1974

The next great bull market of the century began, much like the previous one, after a time of great hardship. In 1949 the economy was in recession. The world was attempting to recover from the devastation of World War II. For 15 straight years, from 1930 to 1945, America had been either in recession or at war. Expectations, predictably, were very low.

The stock market was very depressed in 1949 (see figure A-2). The Dow was trading at about 170, still down over 50 percent from its high in 1929. At that level the Dow was at just one times book value and only seven times earnings. Stocks were so out of favor that dividend yields were well over twice bond yields. Never had stocks been so cheap relative to bonds.

Figure A-2 Dow Jones 1949–1974

Source: Global Financial Data

What caused the market to begin a recovery in 1949? It's difficult to say. Inflation had spiked higher towards the end of World War II; perhaps falling inflation rates after the war generated some optimism. Perhaps the simple absence of war or depression lifted hopes a bit. In any case the Dow did begin a bull market that would last for 16 years. In 1950 the Korean War began but it didn't derail the bull market. That year the Dow finally broke through the 200 resistance level that had prevailed since the 1930s.

The only serious setback during this bull phase was in 1962. After the Bay of Pigs incident in 1961, tensions were rising between the U.S. and the Soviet Union. The escalating political concerns led to a bear market, culminating in the Cuban Missile Crisis of October 1962. Fortunately, the crisis passed and the bull market resumed.

The 1950s and 1960s was a time of both economic progress and psychological healing. Now that the war was over, economic resources could be diverted from building a war machine to meeting the commercial desires of a society looking to rebuild. Compared to Europe and Asia, America was in a position to recover quickly. In many foreign economies, so much basic infrastructure had been destroyed that they had to start from scratch. For this reason, American companies clearly had a global competitive advantage after the war. They could focus on serving the needs of a robust domestic economy with little concern for foreign competition. Incomes were rising, productivity was increasing. Finally, there was reason for optimism.

Although prosperity was once again returning to America, this economy was very different from the economy of the 1920s. The twenties were a time of deflationary pressures and falling interest rates. In contrast, the fifties and early sixties were a time of low but steady inflation and steadily rising rates. In this very important respect, the second great bull market of the century was very different than the first.

In any case, rising interest rates didn't weigh on the market until the mid-sixties, when inflation and interest rates both began to accelerate. In early 1966 the Dow had reached 1,000—which would serve as a barrier to all rallies for the next 16 years! From 1949 to 1966 the Dow had risen 830 points, almost 500 percent. Interestingly, this was the same percentage increase as took place during the bull market of the twenties.

By 1965, valuations were more than double what they had been when the bull market began. The Dow was now trading at over 30 times dividends and over two times book value. The market could support rising valuations while inflation and interest rates were low, but as inflation began to accelerate in 1965, the market entered a long period of deterioration. In 1966 the Dow experienced a relatively mild bear market drop of just over 20 percent. In 1969-1970 the Dow entered another bear phase with a decline of almost 40 percent. And finally in 1973-1974 the Dow was hit with a bear market decline of over 45 percent—the worst bear market the country had seen since the Depression.

Between these three bear phases the Dow did recover to 1,000, but each time it stalled there. There was continued speculation in the market in the late sixties and early seventies. In fact, this era is often referred to as the Nifty-Fifty market, a time when a relatively small number of popular stocks became very expensive while the rest of the market stagnated. These Nifty-Fifty stocks were mostly large technology companies with names like Xerox, Polaroid, and IBM. Most investors felt these companies were so well positioned that they were destined to grow, regardless of the state of the market or the economy.

The bullish outlook for these companies led their stocks to extreme valuation heights. At the peak, in 1972, these stocks were trading at an unheard-of 50 to 80 times earnings.

Investors would soon pay a price for this enthusiasm. In the 1973-1974 bear market, many of these Nifty-Fifty stocks would fall 70 to 80 percent.

Of course the Nifty Fifty were not the only stocks to suffer in the 1973-1974 carnage. Almost all stocks fell as inflation rates of over 10 percent reduced the value of all financial assets. Brokers who survived that era often compare that bear market to water torture. Day after day, again and again, stocks would fall, destroying investors' confidence along with their portfolios.

When the market finally bottomed in late 1974, the Dow had dropped to 577, down 45 percent from the high of early 1973. The bear market had lasted almost two years. The Dow was now trading at roughly six times earnings, 16 times dividends, and well below book value. Though valuations were once again very cheap, the next bull market was still eight years away.

CYCLE #3 : 1982-?

The final bull market of the century would prove to be the largest ever, both in length and magnitude. Valuations would surpass the extremes reached in 1929. But this last bull market would begin, like the previous two, in a period of great economic hardship. In 1982 the country was mired in the worst economic slump since the Great Depression. Unemployment stood at over 10 percent. Corporate earnings (based on the Dow 30 Industrials) had been halved between 1980 and 1982. Extremely high interest rates stifled the economy. Optimism was virtually dead.

When the bull market began in August 1982, the Dow was below 800 and valuations were very low (see figure A-3). The Dow was trading under book value and at roughly 15 times dividends.

While economic conditions were lousy in 1982, an enormous change was underway. Since the mid-1960s inflation and interest rates had moved steadily higher. By 1980, high inflation was considered the primary economic problem facing the nation. Under the leadership of Paul Volcker, the Fed decided that drastic measures must be taken to break the inflationary trend. In an effort to reverse the inflationary psychology, it therefore hiked short term rates (the Fed funds rate) to over 19 percent.

Figure A-3 Dow Jones 1982–2000

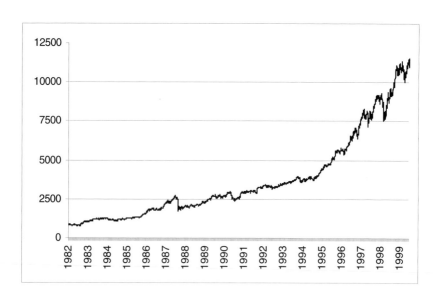

Source: Global Financial Data

By 1982 the tactic was beginning to work. The CPI, which had reached 13.5 percent in 1980, was down to about 6 percent. Long-term interest rates had peaked at over 15 percent in 1981 and were on the decline. Some astute investors recognized that a historic change—and opportunity—was underway. They began to move money out of safe, short-term securities and into longer-term bonds and stocks. This was the catalyst that ignited the greatest bull market in history.

A few short months later, the Dow would decisively break the 1,000 resistance level that had contained it since the mid-sixties. This powerful move on heavy volume was a clear technical sign that the market had entered a new bull market. However, after decades of disappointment, most investors were still very wary of the stock market. It would be a long time before the average investor would again feel confident.

Like the bull market of the twenties, this one was built on falling inflation and interest rates, but because the rates had started so high, the drop was unprecedented. The impact on financial assets was huge: By 1987 the Dow had more than tripled and valuations were again approaching record levels. The world economy was now quite strong and inflation was making a comeback.

A sharp rise in rates in 1987 led to a terrifying crash. In just two months the Dow fell 40 percent. Not since 1929 had the market experienced such a spectacular decline. Many thought the bull market was over. Some thought a depression might be on the way. But to the surprise of most observers, the market and the economy proved resilient. The bull market resumed. By 1989 the market was again making new highs.

In 1990 the Persian Gulf War set off a spike in oil prices to $40/bbl; this was accompanied by a mild bear market and an economic recession that hit the commercial real estate market especially hard. The excessive leverage of the 1980s was being unwound, causing severe downward pressure on real estate prices. The result was the worst banking crisis the country had seen since the 1930s.

The Fed rescued the banks by aggressively reducing short-term rates (see figure A-4). Between 1990 and 1992 the discount rate was brought down from 7 percent to just 3 percent. Effectively, the banks were allowed to borrow funds from the central bank at very low rates and reinvest those proceeds in longer-term government bonds or loans that yielded far higher rates of return. Essentially, the objective was to guarantee the solvency of the banking system while the banks struggled to unload a huge amount of bad assets. The plan worked, but in the process the Fed may have unwittingly touched off the biggest stock market bubble of all time.

Figure A-4 Federal Discount Rate

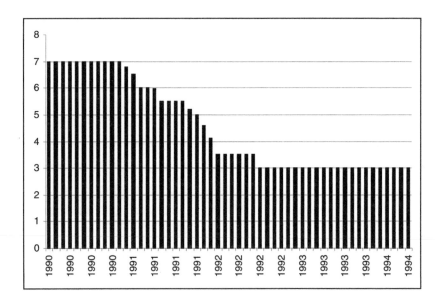

Source: Economagic.com

As short-term rates dropped, investors began to liquidate low-yielding money market funds and buy stocks and longer-term fixed-income securities. Borrowers were able to refinance mortgages and other consumer loans at lower rates, thereby reducing finance costs. All this was a boon to the economy and the stock market. Between 1991 and 1998 the Dow tripled again, moving from 3,000 to over 9,000.

As the market marched higher, one by one all the valuation records set in 1929 were broken. By 1998 the stock market was far more expensive than it had ever been. But as the market rose, investors seemed to care less and less about valuations, or risks. Time and again, bearish advisors were proven wrong by the market's incredible strength. Cautious advisors began to look silly. The market seemed to reward investors chasing the most expensive stocks and punish those who followed a value approach.

As all this was happening, online trading on the Internet was coming into its own. These new technologies provided investors with the tools, and the courage, to invest independently, and Americans were doing so in record numbers. Never before had the market been so important to the average citizen.

By 2000 the Dow had easily surpassed the 10,000 barrier. In 18 years the Dow had risen 15 times! As we enter the new millennium this amazing bull market appears intact and the final chapter of this cycle is still in doubt.

Yet the signs of speculative excess, common to the very late stage of a bull market, are everywhere. Valuations are extraordinary, margin debt is at record levels, momentum investors are celebrating, and rational investors are scratching their heads. Risk is a word that seems to have lost its significance, at least as far as the stock market is concerned.

Perhaps it really is different this time. But history suggests we're simply witnessing the most extreme bull/bear cycle of the past century. The bear stage of this cycle is coming and it promises to be one of the most dangerous in history.

Index